M000210967

PRAYER

— THAT —

CHANGES
EVERYTHING

MARY COLBERT

CHARISMA
HOUSE

permission of Zondervan. All rights reserved worldwide. www.zondervan.com. The "NIV" and "New International Version" are trademarks registered in the United States Patent and Trademark Office by Biblica, Inc.*

Copyright © 2020 by Mary Colbert
All rights reserved

Visit the author's website at marycolbert.us, prayerchangeseverything.org.

Library of Congress Cataloging-in-Publication Data:
An application to register this book for cataloging has been submitted to the Library of Congress.
International Standard Book Number: 978-1-62999-723-0
E-book ISBN: 978-1-62999-724-7

20 21 22 23 24 — 987654321
Printed in the United States of America

☜ CONTENTS ☞

◎ 1 ◎

GOD SPEAKS HIS
PRINCIPLES OF FAITH

IT WAS CHRISTMAS night 2014, and I was at the end of a long, fulfilling day spent with our son, his wife, and our grandchildren. Everyone else had gone to bed, but at eleven o'clock I was still up finishing my labor of love, which had been cooking for and hosting the family. After a few final touches, I left the kitchen looking good for the morning. It was time for some well-earned sleep.

I stepped into our pitch-black bedroom. Anyone who has read my husband's book *The Seven Pillars of Health* knows that one of the pillars of good health is sleep, and one key to good sleep is a very dark room. Don takes his own advice, and he doesn't kid around. The blinds and drapes were completely shut so no light could come in. He even covered the little red or blue lights on electronics with black tape. By this point in our marriage, I think I could have navigated the entire room without the benefit of a single ray of light. Like Don, I appreciate uninterrupted sleep.

I felt my way to the bed so thoroughly exhausted from the events of the day that I don't even remember my head hitting the pillow. My body and mind were way ahead of me. They just wanted to go unconscious.

Then it happened.

As soon as I lay down, the whole room lit up. It went from no light to bright as day in an instant.

"No way," I thought. "Have I somehow slept through the night already? The sun cannot be up right now. Didn't I just come in here?"

Then I heard a voice speak, and it was not Don's. In fact, it was unlike any human voice I had ever heard. Still, my immediate reaction was to wonder, "Did I leave a radio on? Is that the television?"

The voice sounded authoritative and booming, similar to what our friend Kenneth Copeland sounds like when he is preaching under the anointing. But I quickly concluded it was not Ken's voice. It was something I had never heard before.

With a trembling soul, I realized I was hearing the voice of the Father or maybe the voice of the Holy Spirit. I don't know how that all works, but one thing was clear to me: God was speaking to me in my bedroom. Here is what He said:

"Mary! You have been summoned by *Me*!"

Every cell in my body shook with awe and fear. The word *Me* carried with it an earth-shattering power. I knew this was the God who could split rocks with a word and command worlds into being. I can't begin to describe the terror that coursed my body. Like the sound of a train roaring by, so was the vibration of God's very words, the basis of all reality. "No wonder Moses and John fell on their faces when He spoke," I thought. "I'm not sure I will survive this!"

The voice continued: "I want you to get a pen and a pad and write this down."

"God wants me to write something down?" I thought. "He's giving me a message?" But as I was forming those thoughts, He was still speaking without pausing.

"I want you to teach My people the five principles of faith. Write this down!"

The problem was, He didn't stop to let me find a pen and paper! I scrambled around the room looking for something to write with and to write on. I could now see by the supernatural light of His presence. I felt desperate to find a pen because the Spirit of God was talking and had commanded me to write it down. I didn't want to fail my encounter!

That's when I first received the supernatural revelation that He was telling me to write a book. "God has given me a command according to Jeremiah 30:2," I thought, "which says, 'Thus speaks the LORD God of Israel, saying: "Write in a book for yourself all the words that I have spoken to you."' That is happening to me—Mary Colbert. Wow!"

I fumbled through the items on my bedside table as the voice of God continued and as my heart pounded with excitement and no small amount of fear. I finally found what I was looking for just as He declared, "The first principle is…"

CALLED BY GOD

All my life I have heard people talk about their visitations from the Lord. I myself had experienced personal encounters with angels before but never a direct personal encounter with God. Yet I never felt deficient in any way because I am very secure in the Father's love and affection for me.

But I do believe that such encounters are important to establishing a ministry. Paul associates apostles with those who had *seen* the Lord (1 Cor. 9:1). Experiences erase any doubt that God has called you, and they often supply the revelation to help you minister in the years ahead. Don had been called and set aside for a specific work by the Lord, and this was confirmed in multiple ways through a number of experiences and numerous people. I have spent much of my life supporting Don in his work—helping him write books, traveling with him, and being his biggest supporter. There is no doubt in my mind that he was called of God. Don is like a modern-day apostle Luke, and I believe he walks in that same gifting and anointing.

But in our years of ministry, we have also seen well-meaning people launch out before they were called. A friend of mine, Lynn Braco, pastor of Fort Myers Christian Outreach Center, said to me once, "You know, Mary, one reason some preachers don't finish their race well is because some are called, some are sent, and some just took a microphone and went." I laughed when she said it, but there is a lot of truth to her statement as well. She added, "When God calls you, He equips you to finish the race. It's not your own doing. Ministry is not just something to do because you want to. It's a calling." I've observed that pastors who try to anoint their children or a preferred associate to take over their ministry rarely succeed. That's not how ministry is meant to be built. People who minister are supposed to be called by the Father, not by other people. He then confirms that calling through multiple voices and witnesses, not through the decision of one person to anoint him or her.

Having believed this for some time, I had told the Lord, "I will never say I have been called unless You call me. I am not going to be guilty of just taking the microphone and going. I want to finish my race strong, whatever race You have called me to."

Over the years, I have often spoken at women's meetings, prisons, and jails because we are all commanded by the Spirit of God to be witnesses of the gospel and to share our testimonies. Nobody needs a special experience to share the gospel and convert the unbeliever. But certain callings to teach, preach, and evangelize in a more focused and full-time manner must come from the Spirit of God.

For decades I had been completely content to be Don's support, and I still am. I wasn't seeking a ministry assignment. On that Christmas night I didn't see what was coming for me. But the Father knew me better than I knew myself. He knew I wouldn't grab a microphone and "go" unless I had a mandate from heaven. When He started with the words "You have been summoned by *Me!*" it was a joyful, almost playful way to let me know this assignment was straight from Him. He wanted me to know beyond any doubt that He was calling me to share an extraordinary message. Over the next several minutes—I don't know how long the encounter lasted—He put in my hands an amazing set of principles that would change not only *my* future but also the future of a nation through the prayers of many thousands of people.

I had no idea at the time how far this thing would go.

FIVE PRINCIPLES OF FAITH

After God shared the principles He wanted to give me that night, the encounter ended. But I still felt as if I were on fire from heaven. My body shook under a supernatural power. I could hardly walk, but I found my way out of our bedroom. The idea of lying down and sleeping was simply out of the question.

My son Kyle was still awake watching television. Like a kid, he seemed excited that it was Christmas Day and wanted to enjoy every last minute of it. Then he saw me stumble into the living room. I have no idea what he thought, but he looked at me and blurted out, "Mom, what's wrong?"

"Nothing. Don't talk to me. Please." I didn't want to be rude, though my response might have sounded that way. I was visibly shaking, and there was no hiding it. He got up and walked over to me because he could see something had happened. I owed him some explanation so he wouldn't worry.

"Kyle, I don't know if I can talk right now. I just had a visitation from God! Father God just visited me! The King of the universe!"

I barely remember our conversation from that point on. I just knew Kyle was (properly) concerned for his mother, who had just experienced something otherworldly. At some point I returned to my bedroom to try to sleep, but sleep never came. Morning arrived—with its natural light this time—and Don noticed pretty quickly that I wasn't in my typical frame of mind.

"What's wrong?" he asked me in the kitchen. Kyle was looking at me to see what I would say.

"Tell him what happened last night," Kyle encouraged.

If you have ever experienced a supernatural encounter like that, you know it comes with two opposing impulses: you want to share it with everyone, and you want to share it with no one because you don't know how. How could I put into words what had happened the night before? It was so holy, so unusual, so not of this earth that to speak it almost seemed out of place, if not impossible. Now I understood why Moses was on a mountain for forty days getting just the Ten Commandments. Our bodies can't handle the voice of the Father. I think God had to speak one commandment and stop for a few days to let Moses recover!

"I don't know what to tell you," I stammered to Don. "I don't know where to begin."

Then my experience more or less flowed out as I described what God had said. I shared the principles He had given me to share. Don's response surprised me—he began crying.

"Mary, I can feel the vibration of what you're telling me," he said. "The voice of the Father is still in you. This is amazing."

He looked at me with a sense of wonder. Here was his wife buzzing or glowing or *something* with the residual glory of God. I couldn't believe it myself.

There was just one problem to the whole encounter with God. He had said He would give me five principles of faith, but He had only spoken three. Then the encounter had ended.

"You don't know the other two?" Don queried.

"No," I replied.

We looked at each other in awe and perplexity. Why would God announce He was giving five principles, then give just three?

THE TWO MISSING PRINCIPLES

The only reason I had gone back to bed on the night of the visitation was to see if God would share the other two principles with me. It's funny how we behave in these situations. God sovereignly visited me; then I thought I could help Him finish the task! I did nothing to "make" Him give me the first three, and now I was going to help him with the last two? I laughed about it later.

But I remained puzzled. A week went by with no further revelation. Two weeks went by. Still nothing. Three weeks. One month, then two.

"Lord, I can't tell anyone about these principles because You said there were five and You've only given me three!" I cried on multiple occasions in prayer. "They will want to know, 'What are the other two?'"

Heaven offered no reply. So I did what any sensible person would do: I called Kenneth Copeland.

"Ken," I said, "I need some guidance." I could hear the rumble of car wheels on gravel in the background.

"I'm going hunting right now," he said. "I'm in my truck. Go ahead. I'm listening."

I shared the first two principles with him, and he interrupted me.

"Stop, Mary, stop. Hold on, don't talk." I heard his truck door open and close. From a distance I heard Ken shouting, "Glory to God! Praise You, Jesus! Hallelujah!" I could picture him out there on the side of some Texas road praising up a storm. Then I heard him get back in the truck.

"Kenneth? Hello?" I said.

"OK, Mary, go ahead and finish," he replied, his voice still full of joy. "Man, the fire of God's all over me. I feel the power and anointing of God. This is such a word for me!"

I told him the third principle, and he continued to say, "Hallelujah," and praise Jesus while I was talking.

"But here's the problem, Ken," I said. "I don't know what the other two principles are. I don't know what to do with this revelation."

He considered it silently for a minute.

"Mary, I think I know the other two," he said evenly, "but I'm not touching this. This is so holy, I wouldn't dare. When you're ready and you can handle it, He'll give you the other two. Don't hurry. Just relax, and when you're ready, He'll give them to you."

I found that only partially reassuring. When was I going to be ready? How would I relax when I had heard from heaven? Still, Ken's advice was about the best I was going to get, and I believed it was God's wisdom. I had to let my confidence come in quietness and strength (Isa. 30:15) and simply wait on God. He would give the other two principles on His time schedule.

Did I mention I don't like to wait? But I had no choice.

Maybe if I had known what was ahead, I wouldn't have

wanted Him to rush. I had no idea that God was preparing me to play a role in the 2016 presidential election—an election in which prayer based on these principles would become the rudder to help turn America's ship of state in a new, godly direction. In the same way, these principles are meant to revolutionize the life of every believer—erasing discouragement and welcoming power and confidence— because we are praying in agreement with God and according to what He calls faith. Imagine the strength that is available to us simply by praying the way God tells us to pray! That is what we did—and it's what you can do too. Amazingly, these principles made it possible for me and thousands of others to witness results far beyond what we could have imagined.

At the time, I didn't know that soon I would be not only teaching these principles of faith but also living them out in an extraordinary way on the national stage.

2

THE PRINCIPLE OF FAITH
IN CONSTANT MOTION

THAT CHRISTMAS NIGHT, the Father's voice rattled me like a hurricane shakes a windowpane, passing through me as if I were made of tissue paper. "The King of the universe is talking to Mary Colbert right now!" I thought with holy reverence and fear.

"The first principle of faith!" He boomed. "Faith must be in constant motion!"

An explosion of revelation penetrated my being as He spoke. In an instant I saw that faith must be like a river—in constant motion. A rushing river feels like an ever-expanding force, and our faith should be that way too. If your faith isn't constantly moving, it is dead. Like the stagnant water of a pond that breeds bacteria and other harmful things, motionless faith breeds apathy, disappointment, and barrenness. But faith in motion is expanding like the universe. Faith is supposed to be always growing and ever increasing.

A rushing river doesn't stop when it encounters a boulder.

Instead, with all its power, it runs around the boulder or even over it. Faith finds a way to move past obstacles and continue to roll on powerfully toward its goal. Even if its energy or speed is diminished by the obstacle, faith picks up speed again as soon as it goes past it.

Have you noticed that God loves to do new things in our lives and on the earth? He is forward-looking, progressive in His plans for each one of us. He is in constant motion and wants you and me to be in constant motion through our faith, through our love, and in expectancy and readiness for all the new things He is about to do in our lives.

Don and I live in Florida, and we often sit by the ocean and meditate on God's creation. The ocean is a perfect reminder of how the Spirit of God is in constant motion, because the waves never turn off. While you are reading this book, the ocean is flowing and crashing all over the earth. The planet is speeding through space and turning on its axis, and the universe is expanding at mind-boggling speeds.

In the same way, faith works at the speed of God. He is a God of increase, motion, movement, and expansion.

FAITH LEADS TO INCREASE

Let me illustrate with a biblical example you might initially find strange. It is about being productive, increasing, and filling the earth with good things. The Bible says the wickedness grew so great in Sodom and Gomorrah that God made the decision to destroy those cities. Recent archaeological evidence has found signs of collapse-inducing heat, "perhaps as hot as the surface of the sun."[1] I know that it was fire and brimstone from heaven.

One day I said to the Father, "Help me to understand what was so wicked about those cities."

I saw that God's command to Adam and Eve was to multiply and replenish the earth. I felt God was showing me that due to sexual perversion Sodom and Gomorrah were no longer increasing and expanding according to this command. The men of Sodom were so deep in perversion that it disrupted normal married relations.

I wonder if Abraham was thinking about his own desire for a child, a baby to be born to Sarah and him. Maybe he was pleading for the babies and children in Sodom when he was asking God's messengers not to destroy the city if even ten righteous could be found in it (Gen. 18:32). Could it be that God destroyed the cities because no babies or children were found in them due to all the perversion?

When our faith stops producing, stops multiplying, and stops increasing, we are in dangerous territory. Jesus told several parables to the effect that we are given abilities, money, and more in order to produce increase. This is part of what He meant when He told me that faith must be in constant motion. Nothing in the kingdom of God is stale or remains the same from day to day. God is always moving things forward.

TURBULENCE BEFORE UNITY

Motion often involves turbulence. Rivers are not always placid, peaceful places. They have rapids, strong currents, and waterfalls. One river flowing into another is a powerful picture of what it looks like when God adds new things to what He already has in motion.

When I speak at women's groups, I talk about how the Bible describes marriage as two becoming one. I joke that the honeymoon is to find out which one! But seriously, when you get married, you and your spouse are like two rivers flowing into each other. Each of you has your own way of thinking. Many married people discover that when their two rivers merge, in the natural it is turbulent, topsy-turvy, and all over the place. That is why couples often experience relational difficulty in the first year or two.

The same thing happens when God begins a new movement or work on the earth. The existing works often have a hard time accepting it right away. The old and the new works are like two rivers—both good, both exciting, and both with something to give—learning to flow together.

Don't you love how God works?

The benefit comes downstream when these rivers, movements, and relationships become a mighty force. Once unified, these two rivers are much stronger together than they were apart. This is a picture of faith being in constant motion. We are always moving forward, and new things are always being added to the rivers of our lives—things that are designed to make us more powerful in Christ.

A Prophetic Symbol for Forward Motion

God gave me a picture of the power of forward motion when I was just twenty-one and leaving my home city in Jacksonville, Florida, to attend Oral Roberts University

(ORU) in Tulsa, Oklahoma. My father knew I did not have much money, so he said, "I am going to get you a car." I was so excited that the Lord had laid it on his heart to bless me that way—that is, until I saw the car. Sometimes you get tested by what God provides. Are you going to have an attitude of gratitude, or will you murmur and complain?

Dad had gone to the junkyard and bought a brown 1965 Bonneville that had been in a wreck. One door was crushed. The owner of the junkyard told Dad, "Yeah, it will start, and it will run, but the transmission drinks transmission fluid, and the oil is leaking like crazy." So Dad put four used tires on it, gave me a case of transmission fluid and a case of oil, and taught me how to refill these fluids every hundred miles or so.

"One other thing, Mary," he added, "the car's transmission is so bad that you cannot go in reverse. So wherever you pull in on your way to Oklahoma, make sure that you can keep going forward. There is no reverse in this car."

I worked hard to choose gratitude at that moment.

But as I was driving that car across the South to school, the Spirit of God showed me that He had put me in a prophetic automobile. It would only carry me forward. There was no going backward. It was a picture of the power of constant motion—moving forward in Him, growing in Him. Mile after mile, God instilled in me the importance of forward motion.

The prophetic analogy that came from that automobile was so powerful that it remained ingrained in me from that day forth. When I have been tempted to get stuck in some negative emotion or circumstance, some destructive thought pattern or relational response, I remember that Bonneville that wouldn't go backward.

LOCAL CHURCH LIFE KEEPS
YOUR FAITH IN MOTION

After medical school, Don was seeking God about where to do his medical residency. I went into a time of prayer and fasting about this. One day as I was praying, I could see the earth at a distance. A lightning bolt appeared, and I watched it come closer and closer to the earth. It went toward the United States and hit Central Florida. Light exploded out from it and went all over the earth.

"Lord, do you want us to go to Central Florida?" I asked.

He spoke back, "For out of it shall come great light. My word shall come forth out of it."

Knowing this was a word for our situation, I told Don, "I don't know what is going on, but I can tell you that I see us moving to Central Florida. We need to find out what residencies are there and apply."

Don felt God wanted us to pursue this. He was going into family practice, so he researched and found that in Central Florida the Seventh-day Adventists had the top family practice residency in the entire Southeast.

"It'll be nearly impossible for me to get into their family practice residency because of my Charismatic background and the undergraduate and medical school I attended," Don told me. "Only twelve new residents are chosen out of three hundred or more applicants. They are Seventh-day

Adventists and will probably pull residents from their own institutions ahead of anyone else."

Interestingly our beliefs about health, fitness, and diet lined up very well with Adventist practices. In some ways it seemed like a good fit.

"I just believe that, in spite of the odds, you are going to be chosen," I told him boldly, thinking of the vision.

So Don applied to the Adventist school and to several other schools in Florida. God didn't leave us in suspense very long; the Adventist residency program soon accepted him. We met with the director and told him how humbled and blessed we were that they would choose Don to be a part of their residency program and how impossible we thought it would have been!

The director replied, "As a matter of fact, Don, you were one of our first choices. Your sincere faith and your interview helped you more than anything. We could see your commitment to Christ and your lifestyle of exercise and health, which lines up with our beliefs. Though our beliefs deviate from yours in a couple of places, you align pretty closely to what we believe, and we felt as if you were the perfect match."

So God redirected our lives from Oklahoma to Central Florida. We would soon see His greater purpose in that move beyond Don's residency there.

In those first few weeks, we were looking for a church, and one day Don was in the gym working out in a T-shirt that had Jesus' name on it. A guy he'd never met came up to him.

"Do you go to church anywhere?" the man asked.

"We haven't found a church yet," Don replied.

"I know a great church," the man continued. "The pastor is really hard to understand, but he sure is anointed." We didn't know it then, but he was speaking about Benny Hinn.

Earlier, Oral Roberts University's magazine had published a story on the miraculous physical healing Don had experienced in his third year of medical school. Don's photo was in the article. It recounted his near-death experience when he suffered a massive heatstroke and doctors told him the muscles in his legs were dead and he would never walk again. I remember being at our apartment complex and watching Don pull his dead legs up two flights of stairs. We both stood on faith even as Don was confined to his bed—which would be forever, according to the doctors. I remember hearing the enemy scream mockingly at me, "Has God said?" I literally screamed back, "Yes! God has said Don will run and not be weary. He shall walk and not faint."

For three weeks Don had been suffering and not walking. One day I came back from the grocery store and what I saw almost made me drop the groceries. Don was standing in the living room, sweat pouring off him.

"The Spirit of God really came over me, and I heard, 'Get out of bed and walk,'" he explained. He kept walking, and he got stronger and stronger. A week after that we walked into the hospital. The nurses and doctors could not believe what they saw. The pathology report had definitively said that his leg muscles were dead. The doctors took him into a room and measured his thighs, and they were an inch bigger than before the heatstroke! It was a powerful testimony that people all over the nation read in ORU's magazine.

We showed up to Benny's church, the one this stranger had recommended, and we sat in the back with our newborn son, Kyle, to more or less observe. The pastor, a young Benny Hinn, looked out over the crowd, saw Don, and said, "Are you the doctor that Oral Roberts University just wrote about in their magazine?"

Don spoke up and said that he was.

"Come up here," Benny said. We were getting our first exposure to Benny's spontaneity and Spirit-led decision making!

We stood with him in front of maybe three hundred people that morning, and Benny asked us a few questions. When Don explained that he was in family practice residency in Orlando, Benny said right on the spot, "You are going to be my doctor."

We scarcely knew what to think, but it felt right, and it *was* right. We were connected to Benny from that day forward, and watching his ministry grow from that church of a few hundred to expanding worldwide was fully consistent with the great light God had shown me coming from Central Florida. The miracle power of God and His Word were at work in meetings and crusades around the world, and Don was an important part of that for many years. God had indeed led us to Central Florida for a purpose beyond what we understood at the time. Don's medical ministry and Benny's healing ministry began flowing together, creating a picture of the kind of faith in motion God talked with me about on that Christmas night.

Some people lose momentum because they leave the local body of Christ. Maybe a church has let you down. Maybe church life has discouraged you. Hasn't it discouraged us all at some point? That causes some to conclude they can do church and be the church on their own, without connection to a local body. This is a disaster.

What if Don hadn't taken the advice of the guy at the gym about trying out a church, which turned out to be one of the most important days of our lives? How many appointments are you missing by skipping out or staying away from the local body God wants you to belong to?

The churn and spiritual activity of a healthy local church life are two of the main factors that keep our faith flowing. Not only do we gain critical support from believers around us in times of great celebration, heartache, need, and blessing, but the reality of Christ living in others constantly reminds and challenges us to step into greater levels of faith. The local church is a place where you can use the gifts and talents God has given you to bless others. It is in the local church that we provoke one another to good works (Heb. 10:24).

No church is going to be perfect, and we shouldn't expect everything to go smoothly. Remember that constant motion creates occasional turmoil and turbulence—a natural part of our rivers flowing together to become a mighty force. God's biggest works, His mightiest miracles, His strongest movements are always through the church. Make sure you are part of it and keep your faith in constant motion. If your faith has slowed down or stopped, I can tell you with authority that it can flow strongly again. Fresh faith is waiting for you downstream.

LET YOUR FAITH FLOW POWERFULLY

As we go through the various seasons of life in relationships, businesses, family, career, child-rearing, marriage, friendships, and ministry, we must stay tuned into the overarching truth: even when things aren't going smoothly, our faith must keep broadening like a river and remain in constant motion, always growing. This requires us to constantly examine our faith, where we are in life, and how long it has been since we allowed God to do something new.

But many people have faith that is stopped up and stagnated. For some their dreams didn't come to pass in the way they expected, and some have quit dreaming altogether. Many have been hit with multiple disappointments and letdowns, and they feel so disheartened. Their faith rivers ran into the boulders and just stopped flowing. They grew discouraged and quit praying faith-filled prayers.

Others have settled into complacency about expanding or improving their lives. They are comfortable right where they are, and they don't want anything new flowing into their lives—it will mess up their plans! They are like little offshoots of a main river that flow for a short while on their own but then hit a dead end in the terrain, stop moving, and become stagnant.

It doesn't take a midnight encounter with God to show you the state of your faith. He can speak to you right now as this principle is revealed in your life. This revelation is not just mine; it's yours too. That is one reason He told me to write it down—for you. He wants your faith to be in constant motion, always growing in power. If your faith has become dormant, will you put it in motion again?

3

THE PRINCIPLE OF FAITH
THAT EXCITES GOD

WITH BARELY A pause, the voice of God continued to speak to me in my bedroom that Christmas night. How Don didn't wake up, I will never know. By now I was standing by our bed, listening, receiving, scribbling down what God said. I had no idea how to behave in such encounters. I was just trying to be obedient.

"The second principle of faith!" His voice trumpeted (there is hardly another way to describe the power and authority of that sound). "Teach my people to have the kind of faith that excites *Me*!"

The word *Me* felt like an explosion inside me. I thought my heart was going to stop. Again, my thoughts replied to Him, "How do we do that, Lord? How do we have the kind of faith that excites *You*?" The very idea of God being excited by our faith was overwhelming to me!

Instantly, I saw in my mind's eye the Roman centurion coming to Jesus, asking Him to heal his sick servant. When

Jesus said He would go with him to heal the servant, the centurion said he wasn't worthy of Jesus coming to his house. Then he said, "But only speak a word, and my servant will be healed. For I also am a man under authority, having soldiers under me. And I say to this one, 'Go,' and he goes; and to another, 'Come,' and he comes; and to my servant, 'Do this,' and he does it" (Matt. 8:8–9). Jesus' response was, "Assuredly, I say to you, I have not found such great faith, not even in Israel!" (v. 10).

This man had the kind of faith that excites God. Here was the scriptural key God was giving me to support this second principle.

Faith that excites God believes in supernatural results beyond what seems humanly reasonable. If we are believing for something we know we can accomplish with our present resources and abilities, we don't need the kind of faith that excites God. It is probably not even worth believing for. But if our faith attaches to something outside our natural abilities so that there is no reasonable, visible way to make it happen, that's when we step into that amazing place of faith that excites God.

I realized that God has trained me in this in various seasons throughout my life. One of the most important involved finding the man I would marry—or rather, letting him find me.

BELIEVING GOD FOR MY HUSBAND

As a young woman at Oral Roberts University, I wanted the right husband so much that one day I sat down before the Lord and said, "I do not want to date just to date. That is not me. You know the man you have for me, and I ask You to make it plain to me in my spirit. Tell me things about this man so that when I see him and meet him, there will be no doubt in my mind that he is the one You have chosen for me, to be his helpmate."

I sat there in prayer and something came to mind.

His first name will be a nickname and will be three letters long.

I wrote that down. Something else came to mind, breathed by the Spirit.

He will be this tall.

I received an exact height, and I wrote it down.

His hair will be sandy blond in color.

I wrote that down.

He will be viewed as very intelligent.

I wrote that down. So far, so good! Then God really blessed me.

He will have a strong love for Me. He will have a love for playing the guitar. And he will have a strong love for you, Mary.

That last part went right through me. "Aww, thank You for that, Lord," I replied. I posted the list on my bedroom wall, and my roommate noticed it one day.

"What's this?" she asked.

"I was praying about my future husband," I replied. "God gave me this list so I would know who He has for me." That put her on alert too!

A month went by. Two months, then three months. Still I had no sign of a sandy-haired, guitar-playing, Jesus-loving, intelligent man. Then someone introduced me to a guy named Joe. His name seemed to match my first criterion, but he was taller than the height on my list.

"I don't know, maybe I missed some of the things," I told my roommate, trying to fudge Joe into the picture. "This guy does not like to play the guitar, and Joe is his real name, not a nickname."

My roommate talked sense into me when I needed it. "Mary, I just do not believe that he is even close to what God said," she declared. I backed down immediately.

"You're right, you're right," I said. That was it for Joe.

The following Sunday I was at church, sitting in the back and scanning the young men in the congregation, looking for sandy blond hair. All of a sudden I heard the Spirit of God speak to me, "What are you doing?" I froze and could only reply, "You know what I am doing."

It was like I heard Him chuckle, and He said to me, "The man I have for you will find you. You will not find him."

I stopped hunting right then and there. It came to my mind that the Word of God actually says, "He who finds a wife finds a good thing, and obtains favor from the LORD" (Prov. 18:22). Notice that the man is doing the finding! I'm not making a doctrine for everybody out of this, but it certainly fit what the Holy Spirit had told me. My job was to stand on what I'd heard and believed: my future husband would find me.

A month or two later my roommate and I went to a Christian concert. During the concert a student was asked to stand up to model the T-shirts they were selling. He was a bodybuilder, sandy blond, and gorgeous. My roommate was going nuts.

"Where has this guy been hiding from us on campus?" she

asked. We had never seen him before. "Let's go to the shirt table afterward," she insisted. "Let's find out who this guy is."

I agreed, and she started flirting with him while I stood by looking at the T-shirts. His name was Buz, or at least that's what everyone called him. She was finding out all about him and keeping a pretty good flow of conversation up when suddenly Buz turned and looked at me.

"I know who you are," he said.

"Me?" I blurted out. I knew I had never seen him before. "I don't think so," I responded.

"No, no, I went down with the street-preaching team about a month ago, and you were preaching on the street corners to the prostitutes and drug addicts," he said.

He was right. I stood there staring at him and replied, "Yes, I do that quite often."

"I asked someone who you were. Man, girl, you have boldness. I have never seen anybody as bold as you. I really admire that about you."

I flushed an unmistakable red. "Well, thank you," I replied, and our conversation ended as others broke in.

A few days later, my roommate and I were discussing my list while driving through campus when we saw Buz walking on the side of the road.

"Stop, stop! Pick him up!" my roommate demanded. I slowed down.

"Hey, would you like a ride?" I offered through the window.

"Sure!" he said and hopped into the back seat of the car. For some reason, my roommate and I continued our conversation about my list.

"What are you both talking about?" Buz asked.

"Oh, God gave Mary a list of qualities her husband will have," my roommate answered, then rattled off a few of them. She looked at our guest. "As a matter of fact, you fit that list better than anybody we have seen."

She laughed. He looked a little embarrassed. I leaned over and hit her—hard.

"I'm sorry, my roommate is being stupid," I said by way of an apology.

"You girls are funny," was all he said, and he got out of the car.

I found out later that he had told his mom about meeting me and about my list from God. But I was sure he was not the one. I learned he dated mostly cheerleaders, and I was not the cheerleader type. I could not envision this man ever being interested in me.

A few months later I saw Buz again at another Christian concert, and we fell into a conversation for a little while. It was nothing serious, just a light catching up. But afterward I was standing by my car and he came running across the parking lot yelling my name.

"Mary! Mary!" I turned and looked at him.

"Wow, there you are. I finally found you," he said. "I have been looking for you everywhere."

"I finally found you." That phrase struck my memory as familiar. "There's no way," I thought. "Not this guy. It can't be." We talked on and on, but I don't remember anything else we said because my head was spinning. "Oh, my gosh, are you my husband?" I thought. "He does fit the list better than anyone else I know."

We started seeing each other casually, and during our first lunch together, I sat there like a little drill sergeant peppering him with questions. "How tall are you? Do you like to play the guitar? Tell me about your walk with the Lord."

His height was exactly the height on my list. His name was Donald, but he went by a nickname, Buz, that his friends and family back home had given him. It was three letters long. He loved playing his guitar and told me the songs he was learning. He said he was passionate about Jesus and the love of God, and he loved going to vespers. I knew it was not phony. Love for God was a part of every fiber in him. He was absolutely, completely dedicated to Jesus.

I sat there, numb.

That night I told my roommate, "You were right. That is the man God has for me. He's my husband."

Within a year we were married, and we have now been married for more than forty years. People who know us say it is amazing the amount of love Don has for God and for me. I clung to the vision on my list. I didn't go running after second-rate possibilities. I praised God in advance, before I ever met Don, for giving me a great husband. God gave me an incredible gift, and I believe my obedient faith excited God.

USING FAITH THAT EXCITES GOD ON A NEW MISSION

Early in 2015, soon after I had received the principles of faith from the very mouth of God, America entered a political season to elect a new president. This is always an exciting time for our nation, but as the candidates on both sides of the aisle began lining up to try to win their parties' nominations, there was a sense of sameness to it. Senators, governors, and congresspeople who were vying for the nominations were all declaring what they would do for the country if elected president. Nothing was new about this cast of characters. It seemed like a movie we had all seen before.

I don't mean to imply that we weren't in a critical time for our nation. I believe we are at a continual crossroad and that only committed, consistent prayer can keep us moving in a Godward direction. But as we entered the 2016 election cycle, I believe most of us were thinking too small. We saw the future through the lens of the past. We thought only politicians became president. We didn't see that disruption was needed or else our nation would drift into something much less than the greatness to which we had been called.

To be truthful, I didn't even notice this stagnation in our politics. As a dyed-in-the-wool conservative, I was just happy to be done with what felt like eight rough years for our country. I was hoping someone more aligned with my beliefs and values would be voted into the Oval Office and would overturn some of the damaging things that had happened. I was not prepared for God to do a new thing. Not that I wasn't open to it. I just wasn't expecting it. Not many people were.

Then one day my entire perspective on America's future changed when one of Don's patients, a firefighter, walked into Don's office in Florida. I happened to be there that day. Although that was April 2015, the man handed me a prophecy he said he had received in 2011. My first response was gracious but not very enthusiastic. You must understand that Don and I are approached often by people who want us to read their books or listen to their words from God. Most are well-meaning but some are strange. Very few of these words have the ring of truth.

But this one was unusual. As I read the prophecy, it had a weight to it, a rhythm, an intangible quality I recognized as being from the Holy Spirit. In essence, the prophecy said that God wanted Donald Trump to be elected president of the United States and that mighty, dramatic things would happen when he was elected.

As I read this prophecy, the Spirit of God quickened to my heart that this was His will. He counseled me not to be confused by it, even though Donald Trump had not even declared his candidacy. I knew from that moment on that Donald Trump was going to be the next president of the United States of America. This was not natural knowledge or opinion. Like the principles of faith, it came straight from heaven.

The idea of Donald Trump being president would have been laughable to me even fifteen minutes earlier. I knew virtually nothing about Trump except that he had a lot of money and had appeared in a few movies in the 1990s and later. I would no more have thought of Tom Cruise becoming president than Donald Trump. He was just a name floating around popular culture. From a natural point of view it made no sense.

Many people have asked me since then, "How could you have known instantly that this was a word from God?" That's a great question. I have always been extremely careful about accepting people's personal revelations. But I have walked with the Lord now for nearly fifty years, and I have never turned away from Him in rebellion, not even for one day or one hour. I think that's why I have become accustomed to hearing revelations from His precious Spirit to me. I simply know through decades of walking with Him when He is illuminating something with certainty. This was one of those moments.

Politically and culturally speaking, I observed that in 2015 and 2016, many people, especially Christians, had become disappointed and apathetic after two terms with a liberal president. Many had fallen into disappointment and apathy about the direction of our country. But when I read the prophecy about Donald Trump, any complacency I felt went away instantly. I had new hope that God is far from finished with the United States.

Now that I had read a true word from God about who would be our next president, I had a responsibility to start believing for what seemed like an impossibility. I remember the day Trump declared his candidacy. It was all over the news, but few were taking it seriously. My phone rang. It was a friend.

"Mary, did you hear?"

"Yes, I heard. You know what it means, right?"

"He really is running for president."

It was more than that. This day was ordained. "It means the prophecy is now in motion," I replied.

Immediately I began reading about Trump whenever I had time. What was it about this man that made God choose him? What did God see in Trump spiritually that we

Americans couldn't see in the natural? Trump the candidate was—interesting. He didn't seem rehearsed and he certainly wasn't the most articulate politician on the airwaves. His presentation and manner were not as polished as some, and he tended to say clumsy things that got him into hot water at times. But clearly, there was something about him that the Lord wanted to use "for such a time as this" (Est. 4:14).

Then I started hearing about his love for the Jews and all the ways he had reached out to the Jewish nation privately. Trump didn't really advertise those details, and the mainstream media was only interested in airing his dirty laundry and making him look a fool. But after I had done some digging, I realized he had been busy for a long time engaging in behavior I saw as biblical. Yes, he bragged about his financial successes, but that was almost required of him to explain his ideas for the national economy. But all the good and charitable deeds he carried out were done quietly. As braggadocios as he sometimes came across, Trump wasn't really about blowing his own horn.

Trump's rough, unpolished personality seemed to endear him to many Americans. People were ready for someone who didn't sound or act like another career politician. Too many such people in the past had won over the masses with fancy speeches and soaring expectations, only to fail to deliver. The Holy Spirit gave me a scripture to describe him. Proverbs 14:4 reads, "Where no oxen are, the crib is clean: but much increase is by the strength of the ox" (KJV). In other words, if you want the strength of the bull, you have to be willing to deal with the messes it makes. If Americans wanted the strength of a bull, we could not expect the pen to remain perfectly clean.

Even Donald's name was meaningful when considering his divine appointment. I'm familiar with the name's origins because Donald happens to be my husband's name. A plaque on our wall at the health center said that the name is derived from the name *Domhnall* meaning "world leader" or "ruler of the world" (Gaelic *dumno*, "world"; *val*, "rule"). Even more interesting was Trump's whole name, Donald John Trump. John is a Hebrew name meaning "God (Yahweh) is gracious."[1] Trump is a German surname meaning "trumpet" or "drum,"[2] but it's also an English verb meaning "to excel, surpass, outdo," and it's an alteration of "triumph."[3] So Donald John Trump, when pieced together, could easily mean, "World leader under the grace of God whose leadership will excel, surpass, and outdo in triumph."

You can't make this stuff up.

FAITH THAT EXCITES GOD GOES BEYOND THE NATURAL

I was seeing in a fresh way that God loves to use impossible situations and unlikely people to do His greatest works. Think about how unlikely it was for God to call Gideon to do the impossible, a man whose response to God was, "O my Lord, how can I save Israel? Indeed my clan is the weakest in Manasseh, and I am the least in my father's house" (Judg. 6:15). Why would God choose the unimportant and even despised like Rahab, a Canaanite prostitute, and Ruth, a Moabitess widow, to be in the ancestral line of Jesus? In the same way, Paul described the followers of Jesus in Corinth as unlikely people to change the world:

> Not many wise according to the flesh, not many mighty, not many noble, *are called*. But God has chosen the foolish things of the world to put to shame the wise, and God has chosen the weak things of the world to put to shame the things which are mighty; and the base things of the world and the things which are despised God has chosen, and the things which are not, to bring to nothing the things that are, that no flesh should glory in His presence.

—1 Corinthians 1:26–29

God is not only concerned with nations and world leaders but with you and me. Unlikely and common people such as you and I are called to have faith that excites God, faith that believes the impossible, just as the Roman centurion did when he asked Jesus to heal his servant. This man had cultivated big expectations before he encountered Jesus, so his faith was prepped and ready to soar at the moment of his servant's healing.

How about you? What kind of faith are you practicing from day to day? We can have faith that excites God about our children and their destinies or about our grandchildren and the great exploits they will do for God's glory. We can have faith that excites Him for our ministries and careers, for our finances and our spiritual growth. The common factor is that exciting faith is never based on our own abilities or resources.

Natural increase and natural expectation elicit a yawn from heaven. Exciting faith believes for outrageous things. It sets angels into motion. It draws God's attention and invites His abundant blessing. Exciting faith brings supernatural results, supernatural supply, supernatural resources.

I will warn you: exciting faith looks ridiculous to outsiders. It looks illogical to the learned. It looks unwise to the timid. It looks silly to the scoffers. Are we willing to walk in a way that excites God but confounds the people around us? Whose favor and blessing do we want to receive?

When we set our faith on the impossible and unlikely, God gets excited and sends us results far beyond what anyone might expect in the natural. We begin to see supernatural increase, divine breakthrough, and "impossibilities" becoming realities. Hear me closely: we receive by faith whatever we believe by faith. If your faith is small, you will receive small things. If your faith is huge—well, you get the picture. When we set our faith on great things that we could never accomplish on our own, heaven applauds and takes notice.

That's faith that excites God.

My faith was excited by what I was seeing in this unusual potential president, and I believe I was resonating with God's own excitement about what he was going to do for our country. I did not know then that my own role in God's plan would be more significant than I could imagine.

4

THE PRINCIPLE OF
FAITH FOR *THINGS*

THE THIRD PRINCIPLE of faith followed right on the heels of the second as I stood in the bright light of God's presence on that Christmas night.

"Faith is the substance of *things*!"

God said it with such force that I was shaking from head to toe. Suddenly the bedroom went completely black. I looked around. It was midnight. The light was gone, and so was the voice. I just stood there shaking.

"Write it down." That had been his most recent command. So I wrote down what I had heard for this third principle of faith, and revelation flowed to me again. I felt the sharpness and clarity of the Holy Spirit's understanding. I knew that whatever we are believing God for is the substance of a thing. Many times I had read, "Now faith is the substance of things hoped for, the evidence of things not seen" (Heb. 11:1). But that night it came to life. The thing is the object, the result we are praying for. Faith only works when it is attached to objects, to goals—to *things*!

God is focused on what He does, and we are to be focused on what we are believing will happen. Our faith is not to be vague, but specific—attached to some particular thing. Our faith can take shape and become formed when it hones on some *thing*.

God spoke to Habakkuk about events that would happen in the future:

> Write the vision
> And make it plain on tablets,
> That he may run who reads it.
> For the vision is yet for an appointed time;
> But at the end it will speak, and it will not lie.
> Though it tarries, wait for it;
> Because it will surely come,
> It will not tarry.
>
> —HABAKKUK 2:2–3

In the same way, we are to make our vision, what we are believing God for, plain so we can run with it. God will bring it to pass when we have attached our faith to a word from Him.

ATTACHING OUR FAITH TO A NEW *THING*

Don and I grew a lot in our understanding of faith through Don's work with Benny. We were among the first few hundred people at Benny's church. Then he started his healing crusades, which grew dramatically in size and results. Benny asked Don to travel with him to verify the miracles that took place in the crusades.

Benny is a big believer that the natural and the supernatural go hand in hand. We are given responsibility to do what we can do in the way of healthy living and faith. God does what we cannot do in the way of healing. As the result of his own miraculous healing, Don knew from personal experience that God worked miracles. Now God was pairing him up with a man who was taking the message of the healing power of Jesus Christ around the world. It was a divinely orchestrated connection. Don was a teacher and practitioner of natural physical health, and Benny was a teacher of the supernatural. These two streams flowed together into a powerful river. Between the two, God did amazing things.

One day Don and Benny were on a television show together when Benny turned to Don and said, "Doctor, you have such wisdom and knowledge about health. Would you do a little booklet for my partners about health?"

Don agreed to write a booklet called *Walking in Divine Health*. Benny advertised it on his show, and in a matter of days it sold twenty-five thousand copies. There was just one problem: Don hadn't written it yet! He had never written a book and didn't even know where to begin.

"Doctor, I have to have that book," Benny said. "Do something, because I have twenty-five thousand people who have already paid for it!"

Don went to work and produced *Walking in Divine Health*, giving the rights to Benny Hinn Ministries. He insisted that Benny not pay him one dime for it.

"Oh, Doc, I will pay you," Benny said.

"No, no, no, Benny, this is my seed into this ministry," Don replied. Don and I believe in firstfruits, and that book was the firstfruits of our writings. Benny later told us that his ministry received well over $1.2 million in offerings for that book! God blessed that seed amazingly.

One day Benny told Don, "I believe it is time for you to rewrite this book and take it to a publisher. It should be made into a book for the public. Let God bless you and give you a harvest."

That advice led us to the next "thing" God had for Don: authoring medical books. Since that day Don has written more than fifty books, including three *New York Times* best sellers and more than twenty national best sellers. His books are in almost every language around the world and have sold in the millions. Each book was a new "thing" that we believed for in faith. We interceded over each book and stayed faithful to the work of God in Benny's ministry and in our own. Because of that, God overwhelmingly blessed us, just as He wants to bless everyone reading this book. He blesses when we recognize His hand in our circumstances and attach our faith to things He wants us to believe for.

In 2015, to my surprise, God wanted me to attach my faith to an unusual thing—the candidacy of Donald Trump.

ALIGNING OUR WORDS WITH GOD'S WORD

Because of Don's books and the national ministry we have together, Don and I had friends all through the body of

Christ, including at leadership levels. After Donald Trump announced his candidacy, I could barely contain my excitement because my faith had the substance of a *thing* I knew would happen. I flipped through our contact list and emailed every minister I knew, telling them about Trump, the prophecy, and my faith in his candidacy. Soon my Facebook and Twitter feeds became one discussion after another about Trump and the prophecy, plus what our country needed in a new president. I was determined to get the word out about what God wanted to do next in the United States of America.

My goal was to give people faith in the substance of a certain thing I had come to believe—that Donald Trump would win the election against long odds. One crucial way Scripture tells us to exercise faith for things is to speak them aloud. God works by words. Even the blood of Jesus "speaks a better word" (Heb. 12:24, NIV). Jesus is called the Word of God (John 1:1). Every word in the Bible is "God-breathed" (2 Tim. 3:16, NIV). When God created the universe, He spoke it into existence (Gen. 1:3).

The Bible teaches us to watch carefully what we speak. Words have great power to do evil or good. Words can tear down or build up. Words can heal or injure. Words can be beautiful or can feel like sharp weapons. Words are the most powerful tools and weapons in existence, far more powerful than guns, bombs, political power, or anything else in the physical realm. Words are the tools by which we partner with God as corulers of the earth with Him. This partnership is powered by speaking our faith in the things He wants us to accomplish in accordance with His will. How many times does the Word of God command us to pray, proclaim, shout, preach, testify, teach, remember, cry out, sing, and so forth?

I heard someone say, "What if the Bible wasn't meant to be studied? What if the Bible was meant to be prayed?" That's a profound idea, and I believe it—the Bible should be prayed. When you are attaching your faith to a thing, search the Bible and find scriptures that apply to your specific prayer. Just as the kingdom of God is like finding a treasure in a field that is worth selling all to buy (Matt. 13:44), so we dig for treasures in the Word of God that are of infinite value to our faith. As you find scripture after scripture that applies to your *thing*, you will see how all the verses fit together like a puzzle. As you see it taking form, it will become part of you. Your faith will become the substance of the thing for which you are praying.

Let me put it in terms you may not have considered before to build a picture in your mind of what is actually happening when we speak things God wants us to apprehend by faith. First, we know that spoken words have frequencies, like sound waves traveling through the air. Second, we know that "the word of our God stands forever" (Isa. 40:8). Jesus said in Matthew 12:36 that we would give account for every idle word we speak. I believe that every sound ever made, including every word we speak, never actually goes away but continues to resonate throughout the universe. This means that the words of Jesus are still traveling out there somewhere, as are each of our words. That's an amazing thought—and more than a little sobering. Maybe when we give account for our words on the last day, we are accounting for words that still exist and are continuing to work for good or evil.

Speaking by faith, then, is lining up our frequencies with His frequencies and getting into harmony with God, so to speak. This changes how we study and interact with the written Word. When we speak it, we cause the frequency of God to go forth from our mouths. Agreeing with God, we speak forth the things He wants to happen on the earth, and these words combine with the words of others who are praying the same thing and become a mighty river—that constant motion of faith we learned about in chapter 1. By speaking, we literally establish the kingdom of God on earth and overcome evil with good.

This is why the Bible says, "And they overcame him by the blood of the Lamb and by the word of their testimony" (Rev. 12:11). Your testimony in God has the power to actually defeat the highest wicked spiritual principalities. What God establishes in your life becomes the stronghold from which you speak *things* of faith into existence.

ALIGNING OUR THOUGHTS WITH GOD'S WORD

It goes beyond speaking words. Even our very thoughts have frequencies. Some call them spiritual atmospheres. We know that thoughts are powerful because before the destruction of the earth by the flood in the days of Noah, the Bible says pointedly, "Then the LORD saw that the wickedness of man was great in the earth, and that every intent of the thoughts of his heart was only evil continually. And the LORD was sorry that He had made man on the earth, and He was grieved in His heart (Gen. 6:5–6).

Imagine that—the thoughts of man grieved God so much

that He regretted creating humanity. Why would thoughts have such power? Because our thoughts actually emit a frequency. They have substance beyond what we can understand. God mandates that, as His children, we operate in His frequency. This is called renewing our minds. Paul commands that you "be transformed by the renewing of your mind, that you may prove what is that good and acceptable and perfect will of God" (Rom. 12:2).

Notice that the emphasis is on thoughts, not words, and renewing your mind is for the purpose of discerning the will of God. For instance, when we get offended, we think about it, rehashing and reaffirming the offense. We get stuck in our thinking. But God tells us to alter our thoughts and bless instead. "Bless those who persecute you; bless and do not curse. Rejoice with those who rejoice, and weep with those who weep" (Rom. 12:14–15). We change our thoughts by replacing them with biblical thoughts. We need to get on God's frequency and agree with His thoughts, which are higher than ours (Isa. 55:9).

Paul writes in another letter:

> For the weapons of our warfare are not of the flesh but have divine power to destroy strongholds. We destroy arguments and every lofty opinion raised against the knowledge of God, and take every thought captive to obey Christ.
>
> —2 Corinthians 10:4–5, esv

Notice he speaks of bringing words (in the form of "arguments") and "every lofty opinion" and "thought" captive to agree with the words and thoughts of Jesus Christ. He is talking about getting on the frequency of God.

Within your voice and your thoughts are frequencies powerful enough to create and destroy in the natural and spiritual realms. This is the weight of our partnership with the Spirit of God on the earth. This is why we pray continually—not because we have a constant stream of requests, necessarily, but to stay on God's frequency. We do this by cultivating a continually flowing river of praise and gratitude.

It also means that when God speaks a word to us, we meditate on it and speak it out. This was my motivation for sharing about Donald Trump with leaders across the county. I even arranged for the man who had received the prophecy to appear on television and radio to share his story. It was exhilarating to share such a powerful word from God to whomever would listen.

I followed the principle of attaching faith to a *thing*. Faith aimed at nothing will produce nothing. True faith always has an object, a goal, a *thing*. Read Hebrews 11 carefully and you will see that every instance of faith had a thing in mind. By faith God created the universe (v. 3). The universe was the thing. Abraham went in faith looking for that future city (v. 10). Sarah received power to conceive (v. 11). The people of Israel brought the walls of Jericho down (v. 30). I believe things in your life are waiting to be attached to your faith—impossible circumstances, God-given goals and dreams, ideas for business and ministry and for family legacy and generational impact.

What is your *thing*?

For the most part, at that time I was just another citizen with no real power to affect the election beyond casting my ballot. But I had fixed my faith onto a thing and was already feeling the excitement of God in it. Still, I was not immune to the difficult moments of coming to grips with the kind of man Donald Trump had been at certain times in his past.

⤜ 5 ⤛

A CONFIRMING WORD
FROM GOD

THESE THREE PRINCIPLES of faith from God had been rolling over in my mind and heart since the night I received them. Looking back on my life, I realized that I had already put them into practice in many ways. Now I had a fresh opportunity to act on them with my newfound understanding from God.

As Election Day drew nearer, the summer of 2016 grew hotter for candidate Trump as his past deeds and words toward women blanketed the news for weeks at a time. I had to admit that my faith was shaken. Some of the revelations of what he had been accused of saying and doing made me feel physically sick to my stomach.

I began to wonder, then I prayed, "Lord, did I get it wrong? I put my neck out for this guy. Did I miss Your voice somehow?" I paused to consider the possibility that in my excitement I had gotten ahead of the Lord. Had I properly sought His face after reading the prophecy? Or had I run with it too quickly? As questions about Trump's character piled up, I questioned myself. I did what I should have done from the start and set aside time to go before the Lord.

"Holy Spirit, I want to repent for not really seeking Your face about this man first," I prayed. "I can see that maybe I jumped in quickly, got excited, and ran too far ahead. I repent for not asking You to show me clearly whether this is Your chosen candidate for the White House. At this point I need to know if this is from You or not. I have put my reputation on the line with a lot of people. Before I go any further, would You confirm to me that this is Your will?"

I never doubted or second-guessed that the word was true, but I wanted reassurance and the feeling of harmony that comes with hearing directly. After all, He had spoken those principles of faith powerfully to me in an unexpected way seven months earlier. Surely I could request a confirmation of His will in the election.

GETTING A FRESH WORD FROM GOD

Within a day or two I was strongly impressed in my sleep with an unusual idea. In the morning I shared it with Don over breakfast.

"Something happened last night," I began, knowing that it might sound strange. "I really believe that God told me in a dream that He has a message for me in the Belmont Stakes horse race. I feel strongly impressed that I need to watch it."

I must credit Don for his open-minded response. I have never owned horses or watched horse races, apart from a chance viewing or a snippet on the news. Horse racing was completely outside my knowledge and interests—so far, in fact, that I knew it must be from God. I wouldn't have come up with something like that on my own.

But again, I began wondering if someone might have influenced me to be thinking about horse races. I called a friend I had spent time with recently.

"Did you mention the Belmont Stakes to me?" I asked bluntly.

"Huh?" was the bewildered reply. "No, I don't know anything about that."

I felt like responding, "Thanks. I know I'm weird." I didn't care what anyone thought—I had to know if this was God or not.

The day of the Belmont Stakes rolled around, and being human, I forgot to watch! Don and I were busy opening a second office in Fort Worth, Texas, and getting that office set up. We had packing boxes all over the place. We were busy making phone calls, following up with patients, and uprooting everything for a big life move. In the hectic pace of those days, I lost track of the race. On the day of the race, I went to bed as normal, totally forgetting that it had taken place earlier in the day.

When I woke up the next morning, I immediately remembered and thought, "Oh, God, I didn't watch the horse race!" Slightly panicked, I jumped out of bed. I could not believe I missed it! I ran to the computer in my office and typed in "Belmont Stakes horse race." The first result popped up, a big, bold headline. It read "Creator Wins in Photo Finish."

I was staggered and could not believe what I was reading.

The winner of the Belmont Stakes was named Creator—just like my God. To make it even more interesting, the horse that came in second place was named Destin, which I associated with destiny. I clicked the story and watched video of the horse, Creator, nosing ahead of Destin to secure victory.

"Praise God!" I yelled right there in my office. I knew the Holy Spirit was assuring me in His unusual way that God's plan would prove victorious. This was the word of confirmation I needed, and it was very clear to me. It was destined to happen, and nothing—not even a photo finish—could stop it.

"Thank You, Lord! Thank You, Father God! Thank You so much for that message," I praised. "Creator wins! God, You've got this! You're in control of this political race just like You were that horse race. Your man is going to win, and Your victory is going to be displayed for all the world to see! Thank You for this reassurance!"

I then realized with relief that God had allowed the race to escape my mind because His message for me was in the headline. I now had a personal testimony from the Lord that the race had already been won. My excitement and confidence went through the roof because nothing excites God like holding onto a word from Him in faith. I knew beyond any further doubt that God was going to help us put this man in office.

"He's going to win," I told my friends and anyone else who would listen during that tense political time. "In spite of everything that's being thrown at him, Donald Trump will be our next president."

I can't say how many people believed it, but my words

had an authority and a ring of authenticity because God and I were speaking on the same frequency. My words of faith were in constant motion, surging forward toward the thing He wanted to happen in our nation. Each of the three principles God had given me was working in my conversations and my thoughts—and it felt amazing.

It didn't change the polls or the problems Trump seemed to face in those late-summer months. With each day, the possibility of victory seemed to grow more remote. Still, I encouraged others—and myself—with words of faith.

"Trump will win." Because my Creator didn't lose.

BELIEVING THE IMPOSSIBLE EXCITES GOD

Because Don practices medicine, we've experienced many moments requiring great faith over the years, the centurion kind of faith that excites God. One involved a patient of ours, a woman who had fallen into a coma and was about to be taken off life support by her family.

Don and I had just stepped off a plane in Florida when this woman's daughter called, hysterical, begging for us to call her back. Her mother had experienced a massive stroke and hemorrhage a week or so earlier and was in a coma. The doctors wanted them to pull the plug and let her go. This daughter and her brother were distraught because they did not know what to do.

"I feel like we should go to the hospital," Don said. I agreed, though we would have been happy to have gone straight home after our day of travel. When we arrived at the hospital, Don and I stepped into the chapel first to offer the situation up to the Lord. God does not bring everybody back from the brink of death. Sometimes it's not meant to be. We wanted to obey God just as Peter the apostle did when he went into a room and knelt to pray before raising Dorcas from the dead (Acts 9:36–43). I believe he was asking the Father, "Can I bring this person back? Is she supposed to return?" The way I see it, when God's affirmative answer came, only then did Peter pray the prayer of faith that raised her from the dead.

In a similar way, we prayed in the hospital chapel that day, "Father, is it OK for us to pray for this woman to come back?" We felt that we should, but since she was in a coma, we asked God, "Is she gone?"

"No, she's still here. Her days are not over." God clearly responded to us.

The impression was clear to both of us. Now we had something to stand on. We could attach our faith to a thing—the recovery of this woman. Faith does not mean coming in guns blazing to assert your own opinion or your preferred outcome. God won't bless your thing; He only blesses His things. Faith hears the thing God wants to do, then thinks and speaks it until the outcome happens. We were excited to have the opportunity to believe this word from God.

We walked into the afflicted woman's hospital room. As is common for people in a comatose state, her hands were gnarled up. She was connected to multiple machines and tubes. It was not a pretty picture, but we knew this woman was a God-fearing, Bible-believing, faithful servant of the Lord, and He would have the final say over her life. In the corner, her distraught daughter looked up at us and started crying afresh.

"Thank you for coming!" she said. "We don't know what to do. They want to turn the machines off."

A holy boldness rose up in me, the kind that comes when you have a clear word from God.

"Stop!" I said, almost commanding her. "Stop talking like that. Your mom is still here. She can hear everything you're saying."

"She is?" the daughter asked. "The doctors say she's gone. Her EEG is flat."

"I'm telling you, the Father says she's not gone and her days are not over," I said, repeating what Don and I had heard in our spirits in the chapel. "Let me pray over your mother."

I could feel the kind of faith that excites God beginning to redefine the atmosphere in the room. I stepped to the unconscious woman's bedside and spoke to her, using her name, and rubbed her arms.

"I know you're here. Don't be afraid. Nothing's going to happen to you. No one's going to kill you." I spoke to her as Don agreed and the daughter looked on, almost afraid to believe anything positive after being barraged by negative prognoses for days. "Now, spirit of death, I rebuke you. You cannot have her. It's not her time. The Father says her days are not over."

In the natural, her condition looked really bad. The woman didn't budge. Nothing twitched or fluttered to indicate life. Her skin remained pale, and her face stayed seemingly lifeless. But none of that moved Don or me. God had already spoken to us that she was there and that her time was not over. That was all we needed to hear.

Without thinking about it, I turned to the daughter with boldness and said, "In three days your mother will wake up and be fine." The words came directly from my spirit, which was hearing them from the Holy Spirit.

By now the daughter was feeling the change of atmosphere around her. The words we were speaking on God's frequency were resonating with her spirit, and she was becoming overjoyed. She hung onto every word of encouragement Don and I spoke. To her credit she did not fight the word of faith with her doubt. Rather, she entered into agreement with the spoken word. I could feel the situation turning.

"They want my brother to come sign the papers to turn the machines off," she remarked. "He's been in torment thinking he has to kill Mom."

"Where is he?" I asked. "Go get him."

He and his wife were downstairs in the cafeteria, and as we stepped out of the room to go find them, we saw them coming toward us in the hallway. His sister immediately introduced us to them.

"They say Mom's not dead," she said breathlessly. "They say Mom is still here, and that she will wake up in three days."

The son's face registered shock, and his wife, who we found out was an intensive care nurse, folded her arms and looked at us as if we were encouraging malpractice. Irritation billowed off her like invisible waves, but our confidence was not shaken. We were flowing in the faith given to us for a purpose in that critical moment.

After a moment of staring at us in disbelief, the son broke down weeping. "I've been struggling terribly thinking I am going to be responsible for the death of my mom," he said. "But they are telling me I have to make the decision to turn the machines off."

The Spirit of God spoke through me, though Don and I had never met this man.

"First of all, let me just tell you that you do not have power over your mom's days," I replied firmly. "God holds her life in the palm of His hand. He holds all our days in His hands. You could turn that machine off and her heart would keep beating and she would keep breathing. It is not controlled by you, but it will be controlled by the Spirit of God. I'll tell you why. She's a God-fearing woman. God holds all of your mom's days."

The son literally fell into our arms with relief. "Thank you so much!" he said. "I have been so tormented thinking I had to kill my mom."

We had imparted what we had come to impart. There was nothing more for us to do. The daughter hugged me, and as we left, I said, "Call us when she wakes up."

Three days later the daughter called our clinic staff, and our staff notified me. "The woman's daughter called to talk with you, and she's hysterical again," our office assistant said. "She wants to talk to you."

"Hysterical?" I asked.

"No, no, it's a good hysterical," our assistant said, "but she needs to talk to you directly."

We called the daughter. She sounded like a different woman from the one we'd found holed up in a hospital room days earlier.

"Mom's awake!" she said. "She woke up one hour before

three days was complete. She is fully awake, fully functioning, and she is doing amazing, just as you said. As a matter of fact, it's a funny story. The nursing staff came in and told her they could not believe what was happening. They had never seen anything like this. They told Mom, 'You've been in a coma for nearly two weeks. Your muscles will be weak. We don't want you walking around without your walker.' So I went downstairs to get something to eat, and when I came back, Mom was carrying her walker down the hallway! I said, 'Mom, what are you doing?' She said, 'They told me to walk with the walker, so I'm taking it with me.'"

It was the most glorious and praiseworthy result imaginable. I was most impressed by the response of the son and his wife, and the daughter, who decided to have faith that excited God in a thing they believed would happen—the full physical restoration of their mother.

Those kinds of experiences had built our faith many times over the years. So as November approached, I felt increasingly as if this Election Day was going to demand every ounce of faith we had.

◎ 6 ◎

THE PRINCIPLE OF SEEING
THE THING AS BEING DONE

FOLLOWING MY CHRISTMAS night encounter, I was still waiting on God for the fourth and fifth principles of faith that He said He would share with me. January 2015 came and went. So did March and April without so much as a peep from heaven. Then one day I was driving on Interstate 4 to Don's office.

"The fourth principle!" came the voice out of the blue. "Close your eyes!"

I couldn't believe God was telling me to close my eyes. "I'm driving!" I thought. "He must not mean it literally right now."

The voice continued, "When you are able to see that thing that you want Me to do, begin to praise and praise. Your praise will bring it forth."

I saw immediately that this principle flowed directly from the third principle, that faith is the substance of things! Now He was saying, when you can envision the thing you are believing for, begin to praise, and your praise will hasten it forth. Jeremiah 1:12 says, "Then the LORD said to me, 'You have seen well, for I am watching over my word to perform it.'" There is power in the ability to see by faith what you want God to do in your life.

As you envision the thing you have attached your faith to and praise God for it, it becomes part of the very depths of your being. Then you know it will come to pass. At that point no one can talk you out of it. In Romans, Paul says that God "calleth those things which be not as though they were" (Rom. 4:17, KJV). We give God thanks for the outcome that is yet to be, the outcome you can envision. This is the next step in accomplishing the thing you want God to do in your life.

For instance, I can say with authority that in my mind I see revival. I see an awakening sweeping across this country. I see people packing into churches, auditoriums, homes, theaters, stadiums, and public and private places of all kinds—even parks, beaches, and large open spaces. I see people seeking out believers to teach them how to know God. I see the Lord using major movements and ministries to spread this revival across this land.

I see my family participating in this revival in a generational way—our children, our grandchildren, and someday our great-grandchildren. I see this awakening redefining family life, civil life, churches, and schools. I see a reborn America going back to its roots of righteousness and justice. On and on it goes.

What do you see? What can you praise Him for right now before it manifests in the natural?

God knew I needed that fourth principle more than ever

as we began our national prayer call effort. I was about put that principle to use.

Putting Faith to Work

One morning I was praying for the country, the election, and other things when the Spirit of God spoke to my heart. "Mary, I want to tell you something. I am going to do what I told you I was going to do. But if you think this is going to happen without your participation, you need to think again."

The words went all the way through me, and I was more than a little perplexed. I thought, "My participation? I'm no politician. I'm not even a minister! Father, what is it that You need me to do?" I concentrated on His voice.

"Gather My people together to pray," He continued.

"OK," I thought, "I'm willing to do that—but how? I don't have a nationwide ministry. I don't have a television show. I am just a doctor's wife. Yes, I know a lot of influential people, but I have no platform to do anything of the magnitude You are asking from me."

In my humanity I immediately began thinking up scenarios that might fulfill this assignment. Maybe I should go to every Donald Trump rally and pray. No, that's not it. Maybe I am supposed to go to the capital of each state and gather people there to pray. No, that doesn't sound right, either. Nothing had the ring of authenticity.

"Father, what do I do?" my heart cried out. It was as if He'd been waiting for my question.

"Call your son D. J. He will know and will instruct you what to do." The impression in my heart couldn't have been clearer, but it was strange. Call D. J.? My son? What input could my son have for this unusual assignment? Yet, out of obedience I called D. J., not really knowing how to introduce what I needed to say.

"D. J., please don't think your mom is crazy," I started, "but today in talking to the Father, He said He wants me to gather the people to pray across the country for this election. I had the strongest sense that you would know how I can do that. So I'm just going to ask. Do you know how I can do something like this?"

There was a long pause on the other end of the line. Then D. J. spoke with confidence. "Mom, I know exactly what you need to do," he said. "Hold on. I will call you right back."

He hung up the phone. I sat there with the phone at my ear thinking, "I cannot believe he just hung up on me!" He had never done that before. But there was nothing to do but wait. I got up and paced for a while, my thoughts running here and there. I prayed. I fidgeted. I stood up, sat down, and stood up again. I grumbled a little bit. I repented. I waited some more.

Finally the phone rang. Frustration vanished when I heard the tone of my son's voice.

"This is what you're going to do, Mom," he said with authority. "You know many people across this country from all kinds of ministries that you've been involved with, right?"

"Yes," I said.

"You're going to start a prayer chain."

"A what?"

"You're going to call each of these ministers. You're going to tell them you're starting a national prayer chain," he continued. "I've got your 1-800 number here along with your PIN access code. Call every man and woman of God that you know, give them this number, and tell them you are going to all pray together on the phone. Ask them to spread the word in their churches. Every congregation has to know about this. Don't leave anyone out. Not one person. Call them all. Get them on board. Lead the nation in prayer like it's never been done before. Everyone in the body of Christ throughout the United States must know about this number and call in to join the corporate prayer. All over the country, Mom. Every day, at a set time."

"Oh, my goodness, that's perfect," I thought. D. J. had the answer, just as God said he would! He kept talking in his excitement.

"Start praying for Donald Trump on this number, Mom, and everyone who calls in, every caller, needs to be praying alongside you. For the will of God. For His intervention. For the election."

"D. J.," I said, "that's brilliant! Yes! I can do that."

After we hung up, one little part of my brain thought, "This must be too good to be true," so I checked it out. Sure enough, everything D. J. had said was right. There was no fee to the callers or to me. People would simply call the phone number, put in a pass code, and join the group conversation. I had never heard of anything like that before.

"Lord, You are the One who told me to call D. J. You knew he would have the answer, and he did. Thank You so much for leading this right from the beginning! Now, when would You like me to start?"

"Labor Day," the Lord responded, "for this will be a labor of love. Do it every day through to the election. Sixty-five days of people praying for this nation."

"Yes, God. Thank You. What an amazing assignment!"

It had begun.

RIVERS OF PRAYER FLOWING TOGETHER

Within days the Nation Builders Prayer site was online. I called everyone I knew to tell them we would start on Labor Day. I asked them to call in and pray with us.

Then God impressed on me, "I want you to ask leaders you know to host each day of prayer. You will introduce them and serve as the hostess and manager for each prayer call. You will make sure it is done right and that everyone is on the call. But I want different ministers to lead the prayers each day. Then watch what I do."

I obeyed and began calling people to ask them to lead prayer on specific days, right up to Election Day. Some amazing and well-known leaders in the body of Christ stepped up to volunteer. I wanted as many involved as I could find—not just to inform their congregations and audiences, but also to bring in other voices on the prayer calls. I knew the effort would be more effective if the callers weren't just hearing me day after day. I was gratified and encouraged that some of the world's most respected people within the body of Christ signed up to lead prayer.

Our little movement was pushing forward. So I asked God, "Lord, what time of day should we hold our daily calls?" Nine o'clock in the morning came to mind. The Bible makes mention several times about the ninth hour. For me on the East Coast, this meant 9:00 a.m., but for people in California it would be 6:00 a.m., and for people in Hawaii it was 3:00 a.m. I knew this might be a stretch for people in those time zones, but I had to be obedient to what I felt was the right time. So I set the time at 9:00 a.m. Eastern. I knew the right people would choose to join us.

On Labor Day, Monday, September 5, 2016, at nine o'clock in the morning, our first call started as scheduled. Somewhere between one hundred and one hundred fifty people called in.

"Good morning, church!" I started enthusiastically. "This is Mary Colbert! Welcome to the Nation Builders prayer line. We are praying for Donald Trump. We are praying for our country. We are praying for the wisdom of God. Let's enter His gates with thanksgiving! Let's enter His courts with praise!"

This became more or less my standard greeting, and each day the greeting was followed with the name, state, and ministerial position of each guest prayer leader. I instructed callers to shout out the state they were representing as soon as their call was connected, and voices would erupt one after another: "Texas!" "New York!" "Florida!" "California!" "Oregon!" "Nevada!" "Alaska!" "Hawaii!" The callers were almost all regular, everyday Americans—nobody famous, nobody really influential. We had grandmothers, teenagers, working men and women, young moms, young professionals, new Christians, and longtime saints. Every imaginable kind of person was calling in to pray because each loved God and loved this country. They had caught the vision for what He wanted to do in America.

As soon as the prayer began on each call, I muted all callers except for the guest who was conducting the prayer so the line would remain clear of all other sounds. We discovered quickly that fifteen minutes felt like no time at all with that many people on the call and that much excitement. It was amazing how the Spirit flowed through the prayers, leaving each of us looking forward to the next morning's call.

Many others began hearing about the call and wanting to join, but some had conflicts in their schedules. "Please record the call because I have to work," they asked me. "I want to listen and pray later." But God had specifically instructed me, "Do not record these prayers. I am recording these prayers. I don't want people to listen later at their leisure. You are creating an atmosphere at this moment in time, and the ones who are supposed to be on the call joining in agreement, decreeing, and declaring will be there. I will handpick the people who are supposed to be part of this, so don't worry about the others."

It sounded a little harsh, but I had to tell people, "Please understand, I have been instructed by the Spirit of God not to record these calls. These prayers are being recorded in heaven, and this is not something man is doing. This is God's call, and we're doing it His way."

By the end of the first week the hotline company notified me that we had reached capacity for our line, so we had to extend to a bigger, broader line. We soon hit capacity again, and the hotline company informed me they couldn't give me any more bandwidth. We were basically capped at that level.

I told our callers to call in earlier, then even earlier to get their spots on the call, and eventually people were on hold for an hour before the prayers officially started. Anyone calling in close to nine o'clock was rejected by the system. People, prayer groups, and churches found creative ways around the limited-capacity problem. Members of congregations, families, discipleship groups, schools, and neighborhoods met together at locations before the calls and assigned one person to call in as their representative. Then they put the call on speakerphone. This helped their group experience the call together, plus it freed up lines for other callers.

We were seeing the fruit of the principles God had shown me. Our faith was in constant daily motion. We were exercising faith that excited God because what we were praying for was unlikely, impossible, and beyond human ability. Our faith was directed in a focused way at the thing we wanted. And together we were seeing the thing we wanted as being done. It was exhilarating to agree together with heaven and feel the favor of God flowing through our prayers.

Prayer flowed after each day's call ended too. People who had gathered often continued to pray after the call was over. Pastors talked about the prayers during their sermons. Individuals relived certain moments from the calls together, posting items on social media about them. Before long, churches and ministries were starting their own prayer meetings, extending the ministry that God had started through our prayer line. Independently from Nation Builders, most cities in America had several churches in prayer throughout the week at times and places they chose. Franklin Graham started flying from state to state to lead prayer in front of hundreds at each stop, and when other pastors saw this, they were inspired to bring people together for prayer locally.

We were seeing rivers of prayer flowing into each other. What had started as a little tributary was now shaping the political landscape like the mighty Mississippi. It was an instant phenomenon—a move of God as I had never seen. God wants us to be in constant motion, to stir up our faith to achieve the greatness He has destined for our country. He was bringing rivers together to produce a mighty force.

PRAYER IN THE AIR

Hosting the calls got complicated for me a few times when my travel schedule intersected with our nine o'clock commitment. On more than one occasion I was at the Orlando airport getting ready to board a plane when nine o'clock in the morning arrived. Then I had to stand there like a crazy lady and shout into my phone in front of onlookers in the gate area. "Good morning, church! This is Mary Colbert! Welcome to the Nation Builders prayer line!"

But I was carrying out my promise to the Lord to keep the movement going. I didn't have time to be concerned about people who might be upset that I was publicly proclaiming in Jesus' name that Donald Trump was going to be the next president. This was my assignment for the hour.

One morning Don and I had already boarded our flight, and nine o'clock was just minutes away. "I've got to make my call before we take off!" I thought. I spotted a stewardess and rushed toward her with what must have sounded like the strangest explanation she'd heard that week.

"Hi. I'm Mary. Nice to meet you. Look," I said without allowing time for a response, "I'm going to be in the bathroom for a while. You're going to hear me talking really loudly. I'm doing a prayer chain for Donald Trump. God's making him the next president, and we've got to carry him through in prayer."

She looked at me like, "Should we report this lady?"

"So," I continued, "if you hear me shouting in there, don't be alarmed. It's because I'm on a nationwide prayer hotline." I saw Don shaking his head and laughing. He was proud of me, and he was also getting a kick out of this situation.

I made my way to the bathroom with a minute or two to spare before the call began, and I did my best to prepare my mind for the challenge. I knew the flimsy little walls and door were too thin to keep people on the plane from hearing my voice. Even with the door closed and locked, I could still hear Don in his seat chuckling. But it had to be done. At precisely nine o'clock I began.

"Good morning, church! Glory to God! Let's enter His gates with thanksgiving! Let's enter His courts with praise!" I had to wonder what people were thinking in the rest of the plane. "Father, we thank You! We praise You! You're going to do what You said You're gonna do! We worship You, oh God!"

"Stay focused, Mary," I thought. "Don't picture the people outside this door—picture the thousands agreeing with you in prayer across the nation." I pressed on, determined to be a fool for Christ that morning. "We stand in awe of Your glory, Lord! And we know that this morning You are with us!"

This went on for several minutes until I introduced that morning's guest prayer leader. Then I muted my end of the line and sat there in the tiny restroom until it was time to finish the call. My airplane audience heard me rev up again.

"Well, praise God!" I boomed suddenly from a complete silence. "Praise the Lord! Amen and glory to God! I just thank you for that incredible prayer and for your service to this ministry. Tomorrow we're going to have another guest pray with us. Have a blessed day! May the light of God shine upon you, directing your paths and helping you be a light to this world. In Jesus' precious name! Tune in early, folks! We'll see you all tomorrow, same time. God bless you!"

Humbly I emerged from the airplane bathroom and made my way to my seat as if this was what I did before every flight.

"Wow, lady," one of the stewardesses said. "I hope you're praying for us too. Man, that was some serious praying going on in there!"

"Yeah, we're covered," I jested back.

THREE KINDS OF PRAYER

Those of us on the daily call were experiencing the immense power of corporate prayer. I believe it was undergirded by the individual prayer lives of those involved. Let me briefly describe what I mean.

Prayer has an epicenter in the life of each person. We pray for our families, finances, medical situations, and so on. Every prayer life or prayer movement starts with just one person and the Father, alone in his or her closet or place of prayer. In our private place of prayer we are not tempted to make long, flowery speeches for people to hear or to preach at people with our prayers. Rather, we are speaking our true feelings, our true praise in private, for the Father's ears only. Without individual prayer there really is no other type of prayer.

Then it goes a step further as Jesus said that where two or three are gathered in His name, He is with them in their midst (Matt. 18:20). This means a husband and wife entering into agreement or thousands or even millions agreeing together. This is a different kind of prayer that accomplishes different types of things. This is the kind of prayer that reverses dire global situations and turns nations back to God.

We see this kind of prayer in action when the apostle Peter was in prison in Acts 12. The church gathered in a nearby home to pray for his release. An angel took off Peter's chains and opened the gates of the jail. Then Peter went directly to the house where everyone was praying. But the young woman who answered the door couldn't believe it was him because it had happened so suddenly! That is the power of corporate prayer. It brings powerful, sometimes instantaneous reactions. When a body of believers is of pure heart and pure mind with pure intentions, and they gather to pray for the things that they see by faith, then the power of the unified frequency of their prayers ascends to the throne room and causes immediate change on the earth.

The third type of prayer is ministry prayer, which happens when you are acting in a ministerial position. This is the type of prayer Jesus spoke when He healed someone, resurrected a person from the dead, or cast out a demon. Ministerial prayers are not directed to heaven but from heaven to an individual or the spirits involved. Ministerial prayer commands change in the situation at hand and is spoken with heavenly authority and power.

THE MINISTERIAL PRAYER IN ACTION

Our calls involved both corporate and ministerial prayer. On one hand we were calling on God for the thing we envisioned, seeing it done in the Spirit. But we were also commanding life back into a nation that in many ways had lost its hope. This was especially true of Christian voters who had been discouraged for so many years because of bad policies, bad court cases, negative social shifts, and more. The spiritual battle we engaged in reminded me very much of a physical battle I had fought in a real medical emergency—at sea.

Don and I were guest speakers on a cruise ship with John Hagee several years ago. One evening one of Hagee's partners was in the hot tub when he suffered a heart attack and drowned. Don and I stumbled upon the scene as we walked onto the pool deck. People were gathering around the man's body, and there was a lot of ruckus. The cruise ship's paramedics had already arrived and were working on the man, doing their best to shock life back into him and get his heart and respiration going again. Don and I watched them work, then heard one of them say to the other, "He's gone, he's gone. Let's get him up."

Something inside of me rose up. "Oh, no, devil," I said to

myself. "You are not going to humiliate John Hagee by having one of his partners die of a heart attack here on the cruise ship. What a mockery you are trying to make!"

I no longer felt like a politely concerned observer. Instead I felt like an engaged warrior. I made my way to the place the paramedics were gathered around the body, but because the crowd was so thick, I had to crawl toward them. Behind me I heard my husband's voice say, "What are you doing?" I didn't have time to respond; I just gave him a look that said, "Don't interrupt me. I am Mary the minister right now!"

From ground level I literally reached between the legs of the paramedics gathered around the man, grabbed hold of the "dead" man's feet and said, "In the name of Jesus, I rebuke you, spirit of death. Come out of this man!" I knew it was a heavenly assignment.

The man's body jolted and jumped six inches off the ground! It was as if the Holy Spirit put a bolt of electricity through his body. The paramedics leapt back, looked at me, and said, "What did you just do?" In front of all of our eyes the "dead" man regained consciousness!

"I didn't do anything," I said. "God did that."

I stood up and went back to Don. Everybody was watching the man wake up. People were saying to each other, "Whoa! Did you see that?" This was a situation in which the Holy Spirit took over and compelled me to do something. You cannot just go around doing things like this at will. That was the end of my assignment—it was short and powerful. John Hagee did not suffer humiliation because a partner had died while on this ministry cruise, and more important, that man was restored to his family.

On our election prayer calls, I felt we were witnessing the same type of thing—an army of praying people rising at the Spirit's command and speaking life to a dying nation. We had a word from God that we could see taking place, and we were praying and praising God for it.

Through this prayer line, I was putting the fourth principle of faith into direct practice. We were praising and thanking God together for what we could see. We could envision a future in which people across the land lifted their hands and worshipped God. We could see by faith the television news networks declaring Donald Trump the next president. This wasn't imagination; this was anointed, prophetic vision. We could see this was going to happen, and we stood together to pray it into being.

"See the thing you want as being done and praise Me for it."

Yes, Lord!

⟫ 7 ⟪

THE PRINCIPLE THAT
LOVE IS THE FUEL

SINCE THE DAY the horse named Creator had won
the Belmont Stakes, my confidence level had soared.
I knew Trump would win. I bubbled with enthusiasm about the result that was yet to come. In some ways
I was probably insufferable. But I was having a great time.

Confidence is good, but I soon became cocky, arrogant,
even boastful. I knew that the Lord had this election in the
bag, so whenever the opportunity came to prance around
in front of others with this information, I ran with it. As
Election Day drew near, and others panicked as the media
exploded with misinformation, fake news, and hearsay about
our candidate, I floated around on my boastful little cloud of
victory. As far as I was concerned, the election was already
over, and everyone who stood in opposition to my political
opinion was subject to my sarcastic quips. I don't recall intentionally being rude to anyone, but I gave a lot of "all in good
fun" jabs during the many political conversations I engaged

in around that time. I spoke loudly and proudly about the prophecy, my horse race confirmation, and all the things I knew would happen in November.

Boy, was I about to be humbled.

Around late July I went to my husband's office to gather some materials for another trip. I like to read when I fly, so I glanced around my library to choose a book. I saw *The Circle Maker* by Mark Batterson, which I had received with an endorsement request. In it Batterson describes the circle of prayer he walked around his city, claiming the promise he'd received from the book of Joshua, and the transformation that this practice set into motion in his life and in the lives of the people in his community. I had intended to read this book for some time, so I grabbed it and headed to the airport.

Once on the plane I started reading—and was soon reduced to tears. The author's message went straight to my heart. Each sentence seemed anointed to speak right to me. Batterson talked about prayer like few people I had heard. Conversation with God is a privilege, he wrote, not a duty. Christians have access to the coolest friend at all times, in all circumstances. Batterson wrote that trials are joys, not tragedies, as they put us in a position to rely on God's sovereignty through prayers of dependency. As close as I felt to the Father, the book deeply impacted my view of what a prayer life ought to look like. After almost half a century of walking with God in a stable, loving relationship, I felt I was rediscovering on a deep level that my talks with God should be as fun, exciting, and fulfilling as a conversation I would have with a best friend. I knew these truths in my head, but Batterson's book helped me see them again in my heart. *The Circle Maker* called me back to my first love and gave a significant boost to my personal prayer life.

Following this amazing read, my conversations with others shifted from politics and prophecies to prayer. I had to tell everyone about the book. My recommendation and high praise of Batterson's work were the first words out of my mouth for weeks on end. I never let an opportunity pass to share my passion about this new message.

Then the day came when the two messages converged.

I was sitting on my porch, rereading a section of *The Circle Maker*, when a conviction came tearing through my thoughts like a tornado. As a true follower of the Lord, I realized it was not my duty to scoff and giggle at other politicians. It was not my job to crow each time my friends saw their favorite politician's name dragged through the mud. All my political quips and jests seemed so ugly, so unnecessary, so not of God. They were beneath the dignity of the King and His kids.

My mind went back to Interstate 4 on that morning in the spring of 2015 when God spoke the fourth principle to me about seeing the thing we are believing for as accomplished and praising God for it. But then He also told me the fifth and final principle that He wanted me to share with people.

"The fifth principle is love," He said. "You must walk in love, Mary. Love is the fuel, the combustion. Tell My people that shame, blame, guilt, and unforgiveness will block the love you have to walk in. When you walk in love, that thing you want Me to do will be done."

"God, forgive me for walking in arrogance," I prayed, "for

using Your prophetic word and confirmation as a reason to boast and strut and put others down. I am so sorry for responding that way. You are far better than the way I have been behaving. Help me walk in love, not in arrogance. I pledge to walk in faith and love from here on. Thank You for forgiving me for this."

LOVE DOES NOT TAKE OFFENSE

I should have known better. I had studied and taught many times that prayer must line up with God's Word. James 4:3 says, "Ye ask, and receive not, because ye ask amiss, that ye may consume it upon your lusts" (kjv). One very important reason people don't get answers to prayer is because they ask for their own purposes, which James calls "lusts." These can be any kind of ungodly desire, not just sexual lusts. To pray amiss means to pray in a way and for a purpose that does not line up with the Word of God. That is not prayer on God's frequency, on His wavelength. Yet that is exactly what I had done.

How could my pride be on the same frequency as God's kindness, humility, and gentleness? It couldn't. I had cast aside these characteristics of God as I walked in boldness. But we are not allowed to choose the fruits of the Spirit we like and dismiss those we don't. Prayer is not just about God's desired outcomes but about exercising His character in the midst of our praying.

I knew for many years that prayers can be blocked if we walk in offense. But did you know our prayers can be blocked if we are giving offense as well? To be the enemy's instrument to cause others to feel small, ashamed, stupid, unanointed, incorrect, or whatever else is as grieving to God as becoming offended. That's exactly what my bragging and boasting had done. Jesus told us not to lead little children astray (Matt. 18:6). The principle He was pointing out is this: when our attitude offends people and leads them away from God's character or gives a wrong picture of who He is, we are in some measure guilty of leading His children astray. This is a serious thing, and I had been guilty of it.

Let me quote directly from that penetrating passage and draw your attention to the fact that Jesus was addressing pride in His followers:

> At that time the disciples came to Jesus, saying, "Who then is greatest in the kingdom of heaven?"
>
> Then Jesus called a little child to Him, set him in the midst of them, and said, "Assuredly, I say to you, unless you are converted and become as little children, you will by no means enter the kingdom of heaven. Therefore whoever humbles himself as this little child is the greatest in the kingdom of heaven. Whoever receives one little child like this in My name receives Me. But whoever causes one of these little ones who believe in Me to sin, it would be better for him if a millstone were hung around his neck, and he were drowned in the depth of the sea."
>
> —Matthew 18:1–6

Notice that the initiating event for this teaching was when the disciples came in pride of spirit—and asked Jesus to validate their arrogance! Jesus responded by calling a child to Himself and setting him before the disciples as an example of humility. Then He linked pride with causing other believers to sin. Our pride can lead others astray because pride is a form of deception. The enemy will use any error we choose to walk in as an opportunity to cause others to sin.

That's why Jesus' admonition about leaving our gift at the altar is so meaningful for parties on both sides of offense. Notice that Jesus addressed the one who caused the offense, not the one who took offense:

> But I say to you that whoever is angry with his brother without a cause shall be in danger of the judgment. And whoever says to his brother, "Raca!" shall be in danger of the council. But whoever says, "You fool!" shall be in danger of hell fire. Therefore if you bring your gift to the altar, and there remember that your brother has something against you, leave your gift there before the altar, and go your way. First be reconciled to your brother, and then come and offer your gift. Agree with your adversary quickly, while you are on the way with him, lest your adversary deliver you to the judge, the judge hand you over to the officer, and you be thrown into prison. Assuredly, I say to you, you will by no means get out of there till you have paid the last penny.
>
> —MATTHEW 5:22–26

Let me highlight two brief points in this passage that concern what I was learning. First, Jesus was not just addressing anger but also insulting behavior. He said that whoever insults his brother, whoever calls his brother a fool will be liable to human punishment and to eternal punishment. This is what I had done. My attitude and careless words had insulted others who were sincere in their beliefs.

I had, in so many words, called these people fools for not seeing and embracing God's plan to raise up Donald Trump. My behavior fit the parable exactly.

The solution Jesus gave was simple. "Leave your gift there before the altar, and go your way. First be reconciled to your brother, and then come and offer your gift" (v. 24). This puts the obligation on believers to examine ourselves to see if we have harmed someone. If we have, God doesn't even want to receive our worship yet! Nor does he want us to experience the "gift" of spending time with Him. Rather, He wants us to leave our "gift" of time and worship at the altar and go find the person we harmed or offended and make it right.

Reconciliation is not taught much in the church, but it was important to Jesus. When we have committed harm against anyone, the burden is on us to find them, humble ourselves, and make it right when appropriate. Their response is not within our control. They may accept our apology, or they may not. But in God's sight we will walk with clean hands and a pure heart from that point on.

Remember that the Bible says the effectual fervent prayer of the righteous man has great power (Jas. 5:16). A righteous man is one who does all he can to reconcile and seek forgiveness from those he has offended. We don't make justifications, and we don't explain why we did what we did. We just humble ourselves and say, "God has dealt with me about what I did, and I am sorry about it."

In this specific case the level of offense that I caused in any one person did not seem to warrant calling numerous people and giving personal apologies, though I was willing to do so. They might not have even understood what I was talking about. The point was more about me and my heart. Perhaps it was a warning that, if unchecked, my attitude and my words would hurt people more seriously in the future. What seemed proper and right was to confess it to God, tell Don and other close friends about my repentance, and then walk in humility from that point on. In doing this, I obeyed the Word that says, "Confess your trespasses to one another, and pray for one another, that you may be healed. The effective, fervent prayer of a righteous man avails much" (Jas 5:16).

While I am on the subject of offense, we must remind ourselves that it is hugely important not to remain offended. When we hold on to offense and then come before the throne of God to pray, we are essentially bringing Satan with us. He is the accuser of the brethren. Offense harbors accusation in our hearts and turns us into fellow accusers. We have to forgive people and cancel their debts against us. We can't think we can agree with the accuser and have our prayers heard and heeded in heaven. Jesus said:

> You have heard that it was said, "You shall love your neighbor and hate your enemy." But I say to you, love your enemies, bless those who curse you, do good to those who hate you, and pray for those who spitefully use you and persecute you, that you may be sons of your Father in heaven; for He makes His sun rise on the evil and on the good, and sends rain on the just and on the unjust. For if you love those who love you, what reward have you? Do not even the tax collectors do the

same? And if you greet your brethren only, what do you do more than others? Do not even the tax collectors do so? Therefore you shall be perfect, just as your Father in heaven is perfect.

—MATTHEW 5:43–48

The fifth principle is love. God's words on the interstate rang in my spirit, and they are worth repeating here. "You must walk in love, Mary. Love is the fuel, the combustion. Tell My people that shame, blame, guilt, and unforgiveness will block the love you've got to walk in. When you walk in love, that thing you want Me to do will be done."

We must walk in love.

SEEKING GOD IN THE MORNING WITH A CONTRITE HEART

As I released my better-than-thou perspective, my own prayer times took on a greater freshness and tenderness with the Lord. The Holy Spirit had shown me some years before that mornings are special to Him. I recall noticing that right after Adam and Eve disobeyed and fell, the Lord was out walking in the Garden in the cool of the day (Gen. 3:8). What is the cool of the day? It is that time before sunrise. The coolest temperatures are always before sunrise, before the heat takes hold of the day and settles on the earth. Even late afternoons are not as cool as early mornings.

The Holy Spirit impressed upon me that Jesus is "the same yesterday, today, and forever" (Heb. 13:8), and I thought about that. "Lord, You are telling me You are out walking every morning in the cool of the day, aren't You?" I replied in my spirit. I knew it was an invitation. So I began getting up early in the morning to spend time in prayer with the Lord. To my amazement I noticed a presence and peace that blankets the earth before the sun rises. It is different from what you experience in the middle of the night, and it doesn't last long. Once the sun comes up, that special tranquility disappears. I believe the Lord goes looking for people to interact with Him—to pray.

This same example appears all through the Gospels. The Gospel of Mark says:

> Now in the morning, having risen a long while before daylight, He went out and departed to a solitary place; and there He prayed. And Simon and those who were with Him searched for Him. When they found Him, they said to Him, "Everyone is looking for You."
>
> But He said to them, "Let us go into the next towns, that I may preach there also, because for this purpose I have come forth."
>
> —MARK 1:35–38

Jesus received major assignments and guidance in that place of early morning prayer. Luke also tells us, "So He Himself often withdrew into the wilderness and prayed" (Luke 5:16). Even on His last day on earth before His crucifixion, Jesus spent the early morning hours in the Garden of Gethsemane praying.

Why do I say this here? Because when I began to seek

God afresh with a contrite heart, no longer walking in boastfulness, it seemed as if I found Him in a renewed way in those early morning hours. Something about the simplicity, solitude, and innocence of a brand-new day helped bring me back to childlike humility. I can't say it will be the same for everyone, but I believe He was drawing me closer to Himself by pointing me to that time of the day when He likes to be with us intimately. I believe the Lord is out walking the earth every morning, looking for His Adams and Eves to walk and talk with Him.

I encourage you to try it. Go looking for God in prayer in the cool of the day. I often go outside and find a quiet and open view that's peaceful in which to share time with Him. It will become the special place where He speaks to you and gives you revelation and guidance. My favorite place is our back porch with wind chimes—just a few, not too many. The sound rings softly through the air, like the sound of the bells on the priestly garments that signaled that God was pleased with the offering. In this case your offering is a sacrifice of praise and will be time well spent.

Try to quiet your mind and listen to what He may have to say to you. Even more, ask Him to create in you a right heart, to take that which is crooked in you and make it straight. He answers us when we approach with brokenness and submission.

Yes, I continued to believe strongly in faith that Donald Trump would be elected president—but I wasn't called to lord it over others or make them feel foolish. Nor was I to malign other candidates, politicians, and social commentators with my words. God wanted me to reflect His amazing kindness and gentleness. Love is the fuel.

Humbled, contrite, and ready for what was to come, I continued to host our daily calls, and the energy seemed to be building. Election Day arrived with a literal blast of trumpets heard around the world.

8

GOD LEADS US IN TRIUMPH

W ITH ABOUT TWO weeks until the election, everything in the natural looked negative for Trump. But those of us on the prayer call, along with many others, stood strong. I don't remember one word of doubt about God's will being done on Election Day 2016. Not once did an anxious tone or faithless attitude creep in or taint our corporate prayers.

One morning Karen Wheaton prayed, "Father, we ask You in the name of Jesus this day, turn this election around today so that the people will see You are in charge!" We all agreed with her, seeing by faith that it would happen. And on that particular day, we got an immediate answer. An hour and a half after our prayer call, the FBI director announced he was opening a case against Hillary Clinton. To this day people ask him why he did what he did at that moment in the election. We know. It was because more than one hundred thousand people at that moment were bombarding heaven, petitioning God to move His hand that day. When you are standing in the will of God and declaring by faith the thing He wants done, He will use even your enemies to accomplish His will!

That was one of many times during those sixty-five days that we watched answers manifest in the news before the sun had even set. I believe it was because we were operating in the power of faith that was in constant motion, that excited God, that was focused on a thing, that gave us vision to see it as being done, and that was fueled by love. God was using the election to demonstrate this to us, but the principles He had shared were not primarily about praying for certain candidates to win an elective office. I am convinced God was showing us how to partner with Him in every circumstance, at every level of life.

Still, it was remarkable to see such instantaneous results on a national scale.

FASTING FOR BREAKTHROUGH

In the weeks before the election many people on the call felt a shift. We started believing, against everything being reported in the news, that Trump would win by a landslide. Every day someone on the call would come on the line when others were shouting their states and yell, "Trump by a landslide!" Everyone loved hearing that because we increasingly believed it. I remember one morning after hearing a caller announce a landslide again that I saw in my mind's eye the color red—symbolizing the Republican vote—over the US map. I prayed, "Father, I thank You for that vision. I see America red from one side to the other. I see America looking like one big, red country on the day of election. I see Trump by a landslide!"

The vision was spreading between us. We were sharing strength with one another. It was a beautiful example of the body of Christ functioning in the mind of Christ, which is a corporate reality. Everything felt in constant motion, including our faith. Everyone felt excited, and I believe God's excitement was driving it. There was such unity about what we felt the Lord wanted to bring to pass—the thing that our faith was connecting to—that we were seeing it done. Of course, walking in love was not always easy in an occasionally acrimonious election atmosphere, but after God showed me my heart and I repented, I was able to be much more gracious toward political "opponents" and people who didn't see—or want—the outcome I did.

Another feature of those last fifty days before Election Day was corporate fasting. The Holy Spirit had told me to fast, so I took the matter to God in obedience, praying, "Lord, I am asking for You to give Don and me wisdom on this." Then I took the matter to Don, who has published much material on dietary health. He put me on a specialized fast in which I couldn't have any grains, sugar, or dairy. I was able to eat meat, eggs, vegetables, and berries, but no fruit outside the berry family.

As soon as I got the hang of it, I invited our callers to join the fast and told them how I was going about it. I also directed them to Don's website for more information. I understood that not everyone would be in the position to adhere to the same restrictions, so I encouraged them to fast however they could. Fasting is an important part of the Christian's prayer life, and I felt the need to get the rest of the country on board with us.

With the same speed that the prayer chain had initially spread, groups all over the United States joined in to fast along with us. We were not leading or orchestrating the fasts, and I know many believers and ministries felt called to fasting independently from us. We were following the Holy Spirit's leading and acting in a unity that no person could orchestrate.

BLOWING THE TRUMPETS AND ITS MEANING

Right before Election Day the Holy Spirit told me, "Mary, on the day of the election, I want you to blow the shofar at exactly nine in the morning." I had no idea why the Holy Spirit would put that on my mind and in my heart. I did not own a shofar. I was not really active with Messianic Jewish ministry. I had heard of the shofar and knew it was blown on Jewish holidays, but my knowledge of it was negligible. Again, God was giving me something outside my normal framework to do, and its unexpectedness helped to confirm that it was the Spirit of God leading me to do it. Though ignorant of what shofars symbolized, I was willing to carry out the order I believed was from God.

"Listen," I said on the next day's prayer call. "If any of you out there have a shofar, please call my husband's office." I gave them the number and his website information. "Speak to his secretary in the front office and give her your name and number because on Election Day, we're all going to blow them together across the country. So leave your contact information, and I'll call you back."

I had no idea what I was inviting to happen. When I went into the office after that call, the phones were slammed.

Worse, I had forgotten to mention to the girls at the office that I had given people this instruction! Our secretary made a beeline for me.

"Mary, what in the world is a shofar?" she asked.

She was frazzled and the day had just started. Our health center had been open for just a couple of hours, and already we had more than two hundred names and numbers. Even people who hadn't yet heard of our prayer chain were receiving calls from their friends telling them about the Election Day shofar plan, then calling us. I had no idea that so many people owned shofars and wanted to blow them on the Election Day. People were hungry to be a part of what God was doing in the earth in that moment.

I apologized for blindsiding our office staff, then explained what a shofar was and the invitation I had given on the call. "Whatever it is, you have a lot of people wanting to join in!" our secretary replied.

As names and numbers poured in, we had no help besides the women in the health center who took messages. I called each person back on my own. It was incredibly time-consuming because I couldn't just call and quickly give them the information, then get off the line. They were excited to talk about what God was doing. The callbacks took forever, but I made good on my promise to connect with everyone before the big day arrived. Soon we had an army of shofar blowers within our army of prayer warriors. It felt downright biblical!

Still, I didn't really know what I was doing with our shofar plan. God, however, arranged an important phone call. Pastor Larry Huch of the *New Beginnings* television show, who has a wonderful ministry out of Bedford, Texas, that teaches the Jewish roots of Christianity, rang through to my phone the night before the election—the night before we were scheduled to blow the trumpets.[1]

"Mary, I hear you have people from all over the United States blowing shofars tomorrow morning," he began.

"Yes, I do have people lined up to blow shofars."

"Do you understand what you're doing?" he asked. Some might have been offended by a question like that, but I was relieved he was bringing it up, and just in time.

"I don't have a clue, Larry," I said with a laugh. "I have no idea what I'm doing!"

"Would you like for me to come on the line and teach everybody the spiritual significance of the shofar?" he offered. "I can explain what sounding the shofar accomplishes in the spiritual realm and give ten principles explaining what happens when it is blown."

"That would be absolutely amazing!" I answered. "It would be an answer to prayer. Yes, please, please help us with this."

But the next morning, we hit full capacity before Larry could get through on the call. He texted me that his call was being denied because all the lines were full. I panicked, so I did the only thing I knew to do: I had Larry call me on a private office line and speak the information to me, which I then relayed to the listeners. I explained to the thousands of callers that morning that Larry was in my other ear, and I was grateful that they were so patient to remain quiet while I paused at times to listen to him and then repeat his words.

"Let me tell you what happens in our lives and in our nation when we blow the shofar," Larry said to me. I repeated that as quickly as possible. The more he spoke, the more I understood on a much deeper level why the Holy Spirit had instructed us to carry out such a significant act.

"Number one," Larry started relaying the principles, "when we blow the shofar, we are putting God back on the throne of our nation. I believe 1,000 percent we are doing that today as we blow the shofar. It's the announcement of a king or a leader, but it's also declaring that God is back on the throne of our nation. It signals a change in government.

"Number two, it's the sound of a wake-up call. When we blow the shofar, God says He will awaken our nation from a spiritual slumber. As we gather together and blow that shofar in obedience to God's Word, God is going to bring a great spiritual awakening to our nation.

"Number three, it's a sound of rededication. When God gave Moses the Torah, the biblical instructions to the Israelites on Mount Sinai, the sound of the shofar was heard. When we blow the shofar, we are rededicating our nation as people under the Word of God once again.

"Number four, the shofar is called 'the voice.' When we blow the shofar, it calls the voices of the prophets to awaken. The prophecy you are praying about, according to God's Word, will come alive. But not only does God release prophecy, He also releases the gifts of the Spirit, the anointings of God, the signs, the wonders, and the miracles.

"Number five, the shofar in Hebrew also translates to 'the sounds of tears.' It reminds us of what happened when the holy temple was destroyed in Jerusalem. And when we blow the shofar, it's a calling for the rebuilding of the temple of God in Jerusalem by the hands of the Jewish people. It reminds us as a nation to focus on the fact that the Messiah is getting ready to come.

"Number six, it's a sacrifice, as when Isaac was bound but then God provided the sacrifice.

"Number seven, the blowing of the shofar reminds us of how awesome our God is, that no weapon formed against us shall prosper. No matter how big an army comes against us, when we blow God's trumpet, the shofar, that enemy is going to flee because with God before us, who can stand against us? It penetrates walls and brings them down, just as God did in Jericho.

"Number eight, the shofar in English is 'the trump of God.' Isn't that amazing? At the trump of God, the Messiah will return (1 Thess. 4:16). Blowing the shofar is a preparation in our nation for the Messiah to come.

"Number nine, the sound of the shofar is the sound of celebration. It reminds the spirit of our nation that God's salvation comes through Jesus Christ. It reminds our nation that we are a great nation, one nation under God. This was written for the Jews, but it's also for us. An awakening is coming. The reason our nation is great is not because of who is in leadership, but who is on the throne of God.

"Number ten, it's a call to unity in which Jew and Gentile shall become one to make the one new man. The shofar is called in Hebrew 'the shout.' When we blow the shofar, we are shouting for the souls of all mankind to call again upon the God of Abraham, Isaac, and Jacob."

By itself, this list would have been more than enough to convince my listeners and me that what we were about to do was of paramount importance for both the spiritual and the natural realms. But then Larry brought it home with one final thought.

"Let me give you one more thing. The blowing of the shofar is also 'a call to national liberation.' The Jews were not allowed to blow the shofar at the Western Wall in Jerusalem until they won the Six Day War and retook Jerusalem. But in 1967, when God gave His people a supernatural victory, Rabbi Shlomo Goren stood at the Western Wall and prayed for the soldiers who had sacrificed for 'the liberation of the Temple, the Temple Mount, the Western Wall and Jerusalem the city of the Lord.'[2] He blew the shofar, declaring that the city and the Temple Mount belonged to the Jewish people again after two thousand years.

"As all of us from every state gather this morning to pray and to blow the shofar, we are declaring, 'God is back on the throne.' We are declaring, 'We are looking for the Messiah.' And we are declaring, 'Only God can bring national freedom to our lives.'

"So when we blow the shofar, it's not a ritual; it is a supernatural weapon. I believe with all my heart that through all of us gathered together from around the nation and around the world blowing the shofar, we are hearing the voice of God, and God is coming back onto the throne of our nation. God is bringing national liberty through the blood of Jesus Christ."

Larry's portion of the call ended there. At just before nine o'clock in the morning of Election Day, November 8,

2016, people all over the nation had their shofars ready. We had learned the significance of the action. I added one more instruction for the callers: "Don't blow the shofars directly into the phone!" As I called out each state, the representatives answered. Those with shofars who were able to get through on the line that morning totaled around three hundred, representing thirty-five states.

When the clock struck nine, the blast was heard all over the nation. It felt like one of those moments in the Psalms when the foundations are shaken at the sound of heaven. I could imagine the pillars, the roots, the foundations of America feeling that sound, resonating with the blast calling a nation back to God. It sent chills up my spine. I believe blowing the shofars was praising God in advance of the victory.

The prayer that morning went beautifully, and we all felt encouraged that this election was in the bag—God's will would be done. We ended our sixty-five days of prayer calls with great enthusiasm and a sense of imminent victory.

"Trump by a landslide!"

THE SPREAD OF THE RED

Jim Bakker, who had thrown himself into the battle for Trump, called and asked if I would be willing to pray over the phone during his show at nine o'clock that evening while election results came in. He was a nervous wreck because he had put a lot on the line for this election, and now he was in the last hour, with every news station in the country predicting Clinton's win. I agreed to pray with him and his viewers that night by phone.

When the time came for my call, the votes were coming in, and some of the early states were turning blue. Florida, my state, was grayed out because too many votes were still uncounted.

"I know this isn't what You promised, Lord." I prayed silently, looking at the blue states on the news channel's map. I had seen red from border to border. "I know it's going to happen like You said it would, but right now this isn't looking good. Tell me what to do."

As soon as I was connected with Jim, he identified the same issue.

"Mary," he said on the show with the cameras rolling, "we haven't heard from Florida yet."

Suddenly I became almost too distracted to answer because, while I was live on national television, my cell phone started going nuts with texts. Some of them were from Pastor Paula White-Cain of New Destiny Christian Center (now City of Destiny) near Orlando, who messaged me, "Mary, we need to pray. Something weird is going on in Brevard County."

"Jim, if it's OK, I want to pray for Florida right now, specifically Brevard County," I proposed. Jim agreed, so I began.

"I need everybody hearing me on the phone right now to speak over Brevard County in the name of Jesus!" I declared. It felt like leading a prayer call, but this time on television. "We come against you, lying devil! You're a thief. You're trying to steal from this nation the blessing that God has promised, and we are uniting against you right now in the name of God!" I continued my prayer for about five minutes or so and then ended it with a bold claim. "Florida belongs to Jesus! Jesus is Lord over Florida! I am from Florida! This is my state! And I declare Jesus is Lord over Florida! Amen!"

Before my prayer was even finished, Florida was red on the news channels. Everyone in Jim's studio erupted with shouts of praise and applause. We knew that once Florida went red, it would cause a domino effect. We would sit and watch the spread of the red. An air of victory blew over the nation in that moment. Jim was nearly in tears.

"Mary, how have you known all this time that Donald Trump was going to win the election? How did you know? I mean, ever since I've first talked to you—and I've been talking to you the whole time—you've never wavered. You've never doubted even once. How did you know?"

I still choke up when I think of the profound truth the Lord gave me to share.

"Because, Jim, I know my Father. I know my Father very well, and I know He would never call me into a battle that He didn't already know I would win. We are going to win this because this is His battle, and we have done all that He has told us to do. Now we will watch the hand of God do what He does best."

Later that night after the call on Jim's show, Don and I sat on the couch to watch television coverage to see how God would deliver this election to the man He had chosen. We intentionally watched the commentators who were not favorable to Donald Trump because I wanted to see the reactions when Trump was declared the winner. When they realized it was over and that Trump had been elected the president, those commentators looked at each other in shock as they announced that Trump had just broken through the blue wall.[3]

When I heard those words, I stood to my feet and shouted with a voice of triumph. God had done it! His prayer army had stood in one accord to blow the shofars and declare the will of God in the election. Now we were seeing, "Thy will be done on earth as it is in heaven." (See Luke 11:2.)

In fact, the whole world was seeing it with us.

The morning after the election, people sent me videos of people in the streets of Jerusalem blowing shofars. They said they had heard about an American woman leading an effort to blow shofars across the US, and they joined in, taking to the streets to blast their ancient trumpets in the Holy Land. Our little prayer call had served God's purposes just like Joshua and the people of Israel marching around the fortified city of Jericho. We had delivered a blast that brought down walls—blue ones included—and declared national and global liberation from the plans of darkness.

Trump had won the election—by an electoral college landslide.

And it had happened through prayer.

⟋ 9 ⟍

HIGHER FAITH

Sometimes after a major battle is won, the enemy sneaks up behind you with a plan to retaliate to frighten you away from challenging him again. We held another prayer effort during the midterm elections in 2018 (more on that in the next chapter), and not long after that I faced a sudden medical challenge that threatened my life. I was sure it was the enemy's response to our amazing electoral victories.

It began when I was tickling my grandson. As he squirmed around, he accidentally kicked me in my left breast, and boy, it hurt. Within a month I felt something about the size of a pea in that area, so I talked to Don about it.

"It may be scar tissue from where you got kicked, but go get your mammogram and get it looked at." He spoke with his typically confident and faith-filled demeanor, but I detected an underlying note of concern.

Maybe I was hoping it would go away, or maybe I just got too busy to think about it, but it took me two months to get a mammogram. The radiologist stood there looking at the results and finally said, "You know, Mary, I am going to send you over for further tests because I do not think this is scar tissue."

His words shook my world for a moment. I had told myself it was just scar tissue or something else of no real consequence.

"You don't think this is scar tissue," I repeated his words.

"No, I don't," he said. "I think this is something else."

"Something else." I knew from being around the medical profession that "something else" always means cancer. My mother and father both died from cancer. One of my sisters is battling cancer now. I am very aware of what "something else" looks like.

"It may be nothing," the radiologist added to lift the heaviness from his words. "It may just be scar tissue, but I am going to send you over and let them take a look at it."

Still, my head was spinning. "This is not happening," I thought. "Not to me."

I met with a doctor and went through the biopsy process, then waited about a week to get a call with the results. It came while we were at a friend's house on the day before Christmas. I put the doctor on speaker phone as we listened.

"Mary, I really hate to give you this news today, but you need to know, the test results show positive for cancer," he said.

My world seemed to come to a complete stop. No way. No. Way.

"Let's get together and set up a plan and talk about your options," he continued somewhat grimly.

"This is not happening," I thought. My head wasn't spinning

anymore. Instead, it felt as if it were exploding. Four years almost to the day after God had given me the principles of faith, I was being told I had breast cancer.

STANDING IN FAITH FOR OUR MIRACLE BABY

When I heard I had cancer, I built my faith by recalling God's previous miracle in our lives. David did the same as he looked back at what God had done before so he could encourage himself and build up his faith for his current situation.

> I will remember the works of the LORD;
> Surely I will remember Your wonders of old.
> I will also meditate on all Your work,
> And talk of Your deeds.
> Your way, O God, is in the sanctuary;
> Who is so great a God as our God?
> You are the God who does wonders;
> You have declared Your strength among the peoples.
> —PSALM 77:11–14

I thought back to the most serious medical episode in our family's history up till then. It concerned what D. J. and Becky, our daughter-in-law, went through with their second child, Kate.

Our whole family had been so excited to find out that a baby girl was on the way. Kate was going to be our first granddaughter. Three sonograms and two 3-D ultrasounds seemed to indicate she was healthy and everything would be normal.

Becky gave birth to Kate at around six o'clock in the morning, and I soon got a call from D. J.; he was sobbing.

"D. J., what's wrong?" I asked.

"Mom," he said between tears, "Kate is a trisomy 21 Down syndrome baby. The doctor said she is not going to make it." Those were the first words I heard about our granddaughter. Don was sitting at the table with me, and all I could do was hand him the phone. Words would not come.

"D. J., what's going on?" he asked. I was already on my face before the Father.

"Mercy, mercy, Lord, mercy," I entreated Him. "I cry unto You, mercy, Father. Help us to know what to do." At that moment of brokenness and loss, all I could do was rush into His presence and remind Him of His mercy. I was not even asking for something specific. I made no petitions in that moment. All I was doing was crying out for Him to remember His mercy. After Don had spoken to D. J., I got up off the floor and got back on the phone.

"D. J., I'm coming," I said. "I am going to call my sister in Jacksonville, and we'll make the drive together so we can switch off. I don't have time to find a flight. It will take longer, and I might as well just drive."

D. J. and Becky lived in Augusta, Georgia, at the time. I don't know why I felt that my coming would make any difference, but that is all I could do as a mother.

"D. J., I am coming. I am coming," I repeated. It helped me, and I think it helped him get a grasp on what to do next, even if we didn't have answers.

That was the longest seven-hour drive of my life. I was

praying nonstop, giving thanks to God for Kate, standing in the gap, and believing God to do something we could not see. I spoke life into Kate's body. I spoke peace and encouragement for Becky and D. J. I spoke wisdom and divine insight for the doctors. Yet every hour or two D. J. would call with another horrible report.

"Mom, they say that Kate only has one valve and two chambers in her heart, that there is just no way she is going to survive," he announced as gloom tried to pervade the car. "She is too small, and they are saying she will be severely retarded, and that she is probably blind and deaf."

They were giving him the worst possible diagnosis. Each call brought new emotional lows, new battles in prayer.

"Her red blood count is plummeting, and her white cells are attacking the blood cells," D. J. reported as we approached Augusta. "I don't know what the condition is called, but they have given her several transfusions. If her body keeps attacking the red blood cells and gets to a certain level, her brain will bleed out and she will be dead. It will be all over."

I knew he was just repeating what the doctors were telling him, but to hear those words come out of my son's mouth when hours before we had been expecting the birth of a healthy baby girl—it was surreal and shocking. My heart felt torn in two.

Before we got to the hospital, D. J. called again.

"They want to see if they can give her an IV of something called IVIG—intravenous immune globulin," he said. "But it's rare, and they don't know if they can get it."

I knew that IVIG was a solution of antibodies that they

pull from blood and plasma, separate out, and put into a highly concentrated form. It is often given to patients who have multiple sclerosis and other diseases. IVIG is expensive and hard to acquire.

My sister was listening, and she spoke up. "D. J., I am the southeastern representative for the company that supplies IVIG," she said. "I can have them deliver some to the hospital within the hour."

D. J. was amazed, and so was I. Neither of us knew about my sister's connection to this unusual substance that we needed for Kate. It might have been the first good report we received since the birth. Immediately, my sister called her people, and by the time she was off the phone, IVIG was being driven from Atlanta to Augusta. We called D. J. back with the good news.

"Tell the doctors it's on its way right now," she reassured him. "They are driving it as fast as they can."

For me, it was the first time I saw the hand of God in Kate's dire situation. What were the chances that my sister was the southeastern representative for the company that supplied this rare substance that was needed right at that moment for our granddaughter? I almost started laughing.

"God, she is going to live, isn't she?" I prayed. "You are working this out beyond human abilities. Thank You, Father." Joy flooded my heart and soul, almost overwhelming me. I knew that Kate was going to live. I didn't know how, but I didn't need to know how. God was in this.

By the time we arrived at the hospital, Kate was in pediatric ICU. They gowned me up, and I went in to see my little baby girl for the first time. Her body was tied down, and blood gas tests were being performed on her hourly. As a result of this, she had small holes in each of her wrists. As I looked at them, all I could see were the markings of Jesus. "By His stripes we are healed" (Isa. 53:5). Those words ran through my head.

I laid my hands on her chest and spoke to her. "They are saying bad things about you, but this is your Mimi, and I want you to know that you shall live, and your name and what God is doing here shall be known around the world."

I had not planned on saying those words, but they flowed from me as I spoke to my precious little granddaughter. After praying, I left ICU to find D. J. and Becky. In the hospital room, Becky was crying, and D. J. was doing his best to comfort her. My sister, who is a registered nurse, wanted to find the doctor and chew him out for not detecting Kate's Downs on the ultrasounds in advance, which would have saved the family a big shock. I had to talk her out of doing it.

"This is not the time to attack and blame," I counseled. "We are in a battle for a little baby girl's life."

I walked over and opened the curtains to let some much-needed light into the room. I turned to Becky and D. J.

"Listen, I know it looks dark, and I know it appears to be a devastating report, but right now we need to give thanks and praise God by faith for this little girl's life," I told them. "I want you to stand up with me and thank and praise God for Kate, because we do not know what He is doing. But trust me, God is doing something amazing."

They did it. Bless their hearts, D. J. and Becky stood to their feet out of obedience to my request, and through many tears, began giving praise and thanks for Kate's life, trusting that God would do a miracle in her. I declared the Holy Spirit's words spoken through me in the ICU.

"You will be such a miracle baby that your story will be told around the world!" I said. It took real faith to believe it at that moment, but we did.

As encouraged as we felt, Kate's physical situation did not change immediately. Those were probably the darkest and most difficult days for Becky and D. J. to walk through. By the time they took Kate home, she was on a feeding tube and could not swallow or suck. She had had multiple cardiac arrests. By the natural indicators her outlook still looked grim. One time in the middle of the night D. J. had to rush her to the emergency room because she had turned blue. The stress on Becky and him was unbelievable.

But Kate did not die as the doctors said she might. And we still knew God was doing something.

"D. J., I don't understand why this is happening," I told him. "But sometimes we never know the why and God doesn't reveal the why, but we still have to trust Him. Ultimately when we trust Him with our lives, everything, including what happens with our children, is in His hands. That is the most difficult part."

I knew that my words might sound hollow or weak. Trusting God can seem like a fallback position, a last-ditch solution, a cop-out. But it's exactly the opposite. Trusting God is the most powerful thing we can do. We trust Him with the good, the bad, and the ugly. We trust Him even when the results don't turn out the way we want. As dark as a situation may seem, He will take those dismal black ashes and turn them into something beautiful.

Kate was now facing a radical kind of surgery in which they would attempt to create four heart chambers out of two and two valves out of one valve. It was more than complicated; it was highly risky. Success was fifty-fifty at best. On top of that she was a Downs baby, which added another layer of complications.

Kate needed to get up to nine pounds before they could do the surgery. D. J. and Becky fed her, cared for her, and stayed with her around-the-clock, even while raising their other children, including a toddler. During these days, Becky became pregnant again, adding even more to their unbearable load.

Kate's heart surgery went miraculously well, but the doctor told D. J. and Becky that Kate would need major surgery again by the time she was two, and then repeated heart surgeries as she got older because of the complications of her heart.

Don put Kate on powerful detoxifiers to help her detox heavy metals and also gave her the purest fish oil to aid her brain's healthy development. We have learned that God will not do what we can do. God is in partnership with us, growing our faith so we can bear fruit together. We must do our part, then believe in faith that He will take care of what we cannot do. That is the essence of the faith walk.

That's when God intervened. After the initial surgery, the surgeons rechecked her heart. It was perfect. They kept looking and looking. Finally they confessed, "This can't be."

I heard about it from D. J., who called, crying.

"Mom, we have had a miracle. We have had a miracle," he

kept saying. We had expected a miracle, but you never know how God is going to bring it to pass.

Today Kate is nearly thirteen years old and is perfectly healthy. She attends a regular school, takes ballet and gymnastics, and has great hearing and great eyesight, though she wears glasses. You would never know by looking at her that she was a Downs baby. Only when she speaks can you hear a little difference between her and other kids. Otherwise, she is a healthy, happy girl. You would never know what she went through in those harrowing first weeks of life.

Kate was an overcomer from day one.

Now, with a breast cancer diagnosis hanging over me, it was my turn.

BUILDING MY FAITH

Don was numb on the drive home the night we got the news about the cancer. We traveled for a while in silence. I had always told people that when the doctor says "cancer," we should respond, "God can answer." Now I put my advice into practice.

"God can answer," I said aloud, and as I did, I heard the Spirit of God say, "Mary, you do not have cancer."

I turned to Don and repeated those words: "Don, I do not have cancer. This is a lie from the pit of hell. I am telling you, I do not have cancer." It's amazing the confidence you can gain just by repeating what God says to you, even before you fully grasp its implications.

"I agree with you, Mary," Don said. "I just cannot believe it, either. You are so healthy. Your blood work is always so perfect."

Don already wanted other breast surgeons he knew to look at my pathology report and biopsy to get their opinion. So in the days ahead we sent it to them and waited for their response. The devil, of course, was screaming in my mind, "I am taking you out. I am getting you out of the way." It took all my strength to stand on the Word of God and on the principles of faith He had given me four years earlier. Faithfully, I meditated on them.

+ Keep your faith in constant motion.

+ Have faith that excites God.

+ Faith is the substance of *things*.

+ See the thing you want as being done, and praise God for it.

+ Love is the fuel.

I put each of these into practice every day throughout all that was ahead of me. I also repeated His words to me in the car: "Mary, you do not have cancer." In addition, I examined my heart to see if I was harboring offense against anyone. Bitterness is the worst thing for your health and can manifest in many different diseases and harmful conditions. I thought through how some people had done wrong things to Don and me—stealing from us, even as they called themselves Christians. But I was not angry at them. I had forgiven them and prayed for them. Furthermore, I had not hurt anybody or done anyone any harm that I could remember. To the best of my knowledge I didn't need to go to anybody to ask for forgiveness or to be reconciled. Still I prayed, "Lord, if I have done someone harm, please bring it to my attention so I can correct it. 'See if there be any wicked way in me, and lead me in the way everlasting'" (Ps. 139:24, KJV).

Then I examined my own behavior to see if I was out of sync with God in any major way. Was I rude sometimes? I knew that I was. Was I short with people? Sometimes. I could get to the point too quickly, and my personality could be blunt, bold, and strong. I liked to tell people I was a strong cup of coffee. But I could also be gentle, kind, patient, and giving. As I offered these thoughts up to God, I knew there was nothing I needed to get on my face and repent for because my heart was clean. Nothing in my heart was impacting my health or my prayers. I felt His love and affirmation.

During this time of battling the enemy in my thoughts, a complete stranger sent me an email saying, "The Lord told me to send this to you—that you need this message." In the email message was a big banner that read, "The thing that is heavy on your heart and mind will soon go away, and very soon everything will be OK."

I could hardly believe that a stranger would send such a needed declaration for me out of the clear blue. "That sounds just like something my Father would want to say to me in this moment," I thought. So I printed it off, put it in a frame, and set it on my desk. I took it as a word from the Spirit of God for those days. As I walked through the process, I would see that promise and know that He was with me.

Soon the report came back from the other breast surgeons. They didn't sugarcoat their opinions, either.

"Mary, you are going to have to have a double mastectomy," the nurse told me by phone, going over the doctors' recommendation. "And then go through chemo for a year, plus radiation."

I almost passed out. Standing there in Don's office after the call, I kept repeating, "This cannot be. I cannot believe that this is happening to me."

A friend of mine in the office, Rose, happened to be nearby, and she walked in.

"Mary, what's going on? What's going on?" she asked.

"I have just gotten a phone call from the pit of hell," I told her. "I do not even know how to respond to this."

Then Rose did something unexpected and very strange. She started laughing and took her hand and hit the afflicted area of my breast!

"Mary, the Spirit of God says that this is nothing, nothing, nothing, nothing," she announced.

I didn't know how to respond, so I started laughing with her. Nobody had ever hit me there before, and her response struck me as funny. I had no idea how badly I needed someone to break that bad report off me.

"This is nothing, nothing, nothing."

"You know what, I agree with you," I said. "I totally agree with you. It is nothing. This is a lie from the pit of hell. I just do not receive it."

Suddenly, in place of encroaching despair, I had the strength to shake it off. I decided then and there that I had too much to do, too much life to live, and no time to feel sorry for myself. So I refused the invitation to my own cancer party.

Don, on the other hand, was not taking the news well. I could tell that his heart was breaking.

"Don, I am going to be fine," I told him.

"I know you are; I know you are," he said. But I could see it weighing on him.

A Sure Word From God

Don wanted another opinion from Baylor University, which has a leading breast cancer center. So we boarded a plane to Dallas/Fort Worth. As we were flying over the Gulf of Mexico from Florida, I kept praying. Again I heard the Spirit of God speak to me, "Mary, this doctor you are going to see in Texas is going to give you a good report."

Without thinking about it, I turned and blurted out, "Don, I just heard from the Lord. He told me the doctor we are going to see at Baylor is going to give me a good report."

Don nodded and received the good word, but he told me later, "When you turned and said that to me, all I could think was, 'My poor wife. She has no idea. There is no way this doctor could give her that kind of report.'" Don had seen the CT scan and the biopsy. Everything was stacked against me at that point. But I did not know that. All I knew was I would continue to believe that God was in control. Sometimes simple faith is the best kind.

My friend Lindsay Roberts went with us to the Baylor appointment, and both she and Don were nervous wrecks. I, on the other hand, felt excited!

"Mary, aren't you nervous?" Lindsay asked after a while.

"Not one bit," I said. "God has already told me that He is giving me a good report."

She and Don looked at each other, like, "Aw, poor Mary." They tried to comfort me, but here I was comforting them!

Soon the doctor walked in, smiling, his footsteps almost bouncing with anticipation. He sat down and looked directly at me. The first words out of his mouth were, "Well, Mary, I have a good report for you."

Don's head actually flew back, and tears coursed down his face.

"My wife told me on the plane coming here that you would say those exact words," he said. "How can this be a good report?"

"Baylor University is the number one breast research center," the doctor said. "Our breast tumor board meets once a month, and it just so happened that this week we had Mary's tumor up on our slides. We had over one hundred doctors who are involved with breast surgeries looking at your tumor. Yours was one of our case studies."

Who would have thought! I didn't have one doctor looking at my case—I had a hundred.

"Let me just say this," the doctor continued. "If you are going to get breast cancer, this is the kind of breast cancer you want to get. Yours is the simplest and easiest to treat. In fact, I would like to remove it with a simple lumpectomy. I will send your tumor to California. They have advanced tests for studying this kind of tumor, and based on their recommendations, you and I can meet and talk about what to do."

The tumor, he told us, was the size of a pinky fingernail. One side of it had already started to die.

"Your immune system has started to kill it, and the other side is growing so slowly that if we left it in your body, it would not even double in size in ten years. But you still want to get it out."

"Let's definitely get it out!" we all agreed.

He performed the lumpectomy. A week later I went to meet with him.

"According to their studies, you stand a less than 0.01 percent chance of it ever coming back," he said. "The cancer was caused in part by taking too much progesterone."

So it was my fault. It wasn't the enemy who attacked me—I zealously and ignorantly took too much of a certain supplement. Yet God protected me, and in walking through it, He brought me to new levels of faith.

A year later, I am doing great. There is no cancer in my body. But this experience was a reminder that we face battles in every arena of life. Politically the battle was not over after we as a nation elected Donald Trump. And though I would have been happy to become a "normal citizen" with no added responsibilities during the midterm elections of 2018, God had other plans for me.

∼ 10 ∼

PRAYING WITH POWER

AFTER THE 2016 election I thought my assignment leading a national prayer call was over. But God had other plans. He wanted to teach us to pray with even greater authority and with specific heavenly guidance. What we had experienced so far was just a warm-up for some of the lessons and surprises that were ahead.

Still, I resisted when those who had participated in our calls contacted me to say, "Are you going to continue the prayer calls? We have to continue praying!" I agreed that people needed to keep praying for President Donald Trump, for the Supreme Court, for Congress, and for revival in our nation. Indeed, Christians everywhere had awakened to the fact that our country's leadership would not succeed unless the citizenry lifted them up continually in prayer. This needed to happen individually, in groups, in churches, and in families. As a result of the election, there seemed to be a much greater understanding among Christians that prayer was critical to turning our nation around.

But to be honest, I didn't want to lead another prayer effort

113

during the midterm elections. It is a huge commitment, especially when it takes place every day. My life was full enough that I didn't feel like taking on this major responsibility unless God really wanted me to. And I wasn't asking Him for it.

Still, a number of voices continued to speak this assignment to me. Don thought I should rally people and lead a prayer call in 2018, and so did other people I respect. I let their words and exhortations go past me. I didn't want to budge on the matter. Then one day a man we did not know drove from Michigan to my husband's office in Orlando, Florida. He walked in unannounced and said, "I came to talk to Mary Colbert." I happened to be available for a moment, so I went out to meet him and see what he wanted.

"I was on your prayer call for Donald Trump last election," he said, "and I felt the Lord sent me down here to tell you, 'You need to continue doing this.'"

His words were like a splash of cold water. I stood there not wanting to acknowledge the power I felt behind them.

"Sir," I said, "why do you think God would ask me to continue doing this?"

"Because we need it, and the people need to keep praying," he responded.

Again, his words had a force from heaven.

"So why don't you do it?" I retorted. Like I said, a strong cup of coffee.

But I knew his message was for me. I thanked him graciously for obeying the Lord and driving all the way down to see us. He had gone above and beyond the call of duty to deliver a much-needed message.

I couldn't ignore the obvious anymore. As I meditated on what I should do, the conviction grew stronger in my heart that I should lead a prayer call for the midterms. I guess I was catching up with what everyone around me already knew. Immediately, before I could plan it in my own understanding, I sought the Lord about what a prayer effort should look like this time. I knew better than to repeat the same thing God blessed last time. Whenever you try to use the same recipe, the results come out stale. God is into serving fresh manna.

We need to seek God fresh each time we need direction. In the wilderness God told Moses to strike a rock to bring water forth from it to quench the Israelite's thirst (Exod. 17:6). The next time, God told Moses to speak to the rock to bring forth water because He was doing a new thing (Num. 20:8).

David knew he needed to consult with God each time he went to battle. When the Philistines came to threaten Israel, David inquired of the Lord about whether he should go fight them (2 Sam. 5:19). He didn't just assume he should go. The Lord instructed him to go and gave him a great victory. Later the Philistines came again to the same place to attack Israel, and David sought the Lord anew. This time the Lord gave him a new battle plan (2 Sam. 22–25). We need to seek God for every new thing, and I knew that.

"Lord, if you want me to do this, what should I do? How should I do it?" I asked Him morning after morning in the cool of the day.

Soon I felt His guidance. In 2016 we had invited big names from major ministries to lead the prayer calls each day. Their participation was a huge reason the calls increased so fast. This time I sensed that the Lord wanted regular people, not big names. He wanted a truly grassroots movement.

"Start with the As and go through the alphabet, praying for each state in the Union, from Alabama to Wyoming," He spoke to my heart. "It will be fifty states of jubilee. Announce what you are doing by email and ask for intercessors from different states to contact you. They will then team up with other intercessors in their states. They will hear from Me and lead the corporate prayers for their state."

I found this approach refreshing and highly democratic. Instead of a top-down approach to praying, we were freeing the Holy Spirit to raise the prayer movement up starting at the ground-level perspective of intercessors in each state.

"You have to do your homework this time, folks," I told our participants as we began to assemble. "This won't be me or anyone else telling you what to pray or for whom to pray. God has given you the authority over your state. I live in Florida. I don't have authority over anywhere else—but you do. It's important that we find praying people in our states to stand in agreement with about this election."

We started the daily call on Labor Day again. The fifty-day challenge started a couple weeks later. Individuals from each state led the prayer on the day we prayed for their state. Within a short time it grew even larger than the 2016 prayer call. In fact, it reached twice the size. People from many other countries streamed the call through the internet and prayed with us, agreeing for the United States to come back to God.

God was doing something again.

PRAYING FOR THE OPPOSITION

Halfway through the effort the Holy Spirit spoke a very unexpected word to me during one of the calls. "I want you to tell people on the prayer call that they are not going to get everything they want this time."

"Oh, boy, Lord. Help me out here," I responded. "Tell me what You mean."

"I know you have given up on the Democratic Party, but I haven't." His words surprised me more than a little. "I want you to command the people to pray for the Democratic Party to come back to Me," He said.

"Lord, people won't be happy to hear this," I said. "You know the emails and phone calls I will get. I can hear them now."

But He didn't change His mind.

"I established the Constitution with checks and balances, and whenever one party gets into power, it becomes corrupt," He seemed to impress on me. "The parties are a balance to keep everybody in check. The Democratic Party has gone so far away from what it should be that their checks and balances are gone. But there are people in the Democratic Party who love Me and who have been bullied so that their voices are silenced. Pray that they will rise up and take back their party for Me."

God's word to me reminded me of the words the Lord spoke to Joshua before the Israelites defeated Jericho:

> And it came to pass, when Joshua was by Jericho, that
> he lifted his eyes and looked, and behold, a Man stood
> opposite him with His sword drawn in His hand. And

> Joshua went to Him and said to Him, "Are You for us or for our adversaries?"
>
> So He said, "No, but as Commander of the army of the Lord I have now come."
>
> And Joshua fell on his face to the earth and worshiped, and said to Him, "What does my Lord say to His servant?"
>
> Then the Commander of the Lord's army said to Joshua, "Take your sandal off your foot, for the place where you stand is holy." And Joshua did so.
>
> —Joshua 5:13–15

Sometimes when we have an instruction from God, we believe God is on our side. Joshua and the Israelites were acting on God's word, but God had a larger plan. The commander of the Lord's army had his own battle plan that was much grander than the instructions He gave Joshua and the Israelites.

We, too, must remember that when we obey God, we don't necessarily have the whole picture. God loves everyone and is always working for the good of all people. We are grateful to do our part.

I spoke that word about praying for the Democratic Party on our call, and to my surprise people were not upset. Rather, they were grieved that something of value—a viable, godly Democratic Party—had gone so far away from God in its policies. God was surprising us again with His merciful heart not just for one political party but for people of all political perspectives. He likes godly diversity. Rather than seeing it as praying for our opposition in the political sphere, we now understood that we were praying for wayward brothers and sisters.

Amazingly, as soon as we agreed with the Lord about the future of that party, people began to come into our office who had once been Democrats but had been driven from the party by its radical agenda. Through tears they told us, "It has broken my heart what has happened to the Democratic Party. Thank you for praying that its true character will be restored."

To believe God for a righteous Democratic Party certainly took faith that excites God. To many of us it seemed like an impossible task. But that's what God likes—to do things that man cannot make happen. Our faith felt big as we agreed with God for everybody on the political spectrum, not just our side. He wanted our faith and our prayers to go beyond our limited political goals. He wanted to heal and turn an entire nation.

So we prayed, "God, You have the ability to turn everybody in this nation back to You. You can remove blinders and reverse policies and give godly wisdom in the place of dark counsel. We are asking You to turn the Democratic Party and this entire country back to You!"

It felt awesome.

FEARSOME RESULTS AND NEW PRINCIPLES

During this time of praying for one state per day for fifty days of jubilee, we came to the day we would pray for Nevada. None of us who were on that call will ever forget it. The intercessors in Nevada prayed so powerfully that the presence of God was palpable to everyone listening. People were talking about it afterward saying, "Did you feel that?" God's presence flooded the phone lines as those intercessors pleaded for their state. One woman in particular prayed, "Father, today we beseech You to remove the wicked man and woman from our presence and their rule over us! We need You to remove them where we cannot. You know their names." The call left us in awe of what we had heard and sensed. It was direct partnership and agreement with heaven.

The next morning we woke up to headlines that said that this Nevada brothel owner and candidate for the state assembly had died overnight of a heart attack.[1] This man was a Republican who wrote a book called *The Art of the Pimp*.

When our call began that morning, the line was absolutely buzzing. "Did you see the headlines in Nevada? Do you remember those prayers yesterday?" To say we felt holy fear and reverence of God's power would be an understatement. Our cry had been for the wicked man to be removed from among us. God had acted within hours of our cry. He had done it in response to the prayers of people in Nevada itself. It was as if He had given them authority to cast down strongholds of wickedness in their own state.

I believe that was a preview of the kind of authority and specific prayer guidance the Holy Spirit is bringing back to the body of Christ. Buckle up and get ready for immediate answers and powerful, awe-inspiring prayers that directly affect our politics and society. I am convinced it will be a greater expression of heavenly authority than America has witnessed in generations.

On the call for Arizona, I heard from the Lord during the call itself. I prayed what I heard aloud, saying, "I thank

You that I feel confirmed in my spirit that the Republican woman running for US senator will be senator."

We became confident in the outcome of that race from that point on, but on Election Day the Arizona US senate race went to a runoff—and the Democratic candidate won. I was confused—more than confused, upset—because I felt I had heard clearly from God. People called me to say, "I remember you said the Lord told you this other woman would be senator. We trust that you hear from God. What happened?"

I didn't know what to say.

"Lord, I know what I heard that morning," I cried out in prayer. "How could I have been so deceived and misled people?"

The answer arrived fewer than thirty days later when Arizona's governor appointed the Republican candidate I thought would win the election to fill John McCain's seat after his death. The word God had given me was not that she would win the race, but that she would be the senator from Arizona. Indeed, she was! It was a good example of how specific God is when He speaks to us.

Although the current crop of pro-life Democrats is fairly small, five of six kept their seats in the House and Senate—two in the midst of close reelection campaigns. It seemed God was answering our prayers for a revitalized, righteous Democratic Party.

More importantly, God was showing us how to pray His specific will, which produces power in every situation. God was revealing more life examples in addition to those He had given to me on Christmas night. Faith prays specifically, based on guidance from the Holy Spirit, and these prayers are powerful, even fearsome. He also really meant it when He said to pray for our enemies, for our opposition. God is kind and generous toward those who oppose Him. If we lose that perspective, we can see prayer only as a tool to impose our preferred outcome on a situation. That is not the heart of God, who is always working to bring all people into a greater revelation of who He is.

As we moved forward, I understood that prayer is not limited to election cycles but is a lifetime journey of learning and doing that happens in close partnership with the Holy Spirit. Love is the fuel, and love always draws us closer to Him. There is no end to what He wants to teach us.

❀ 11 ❀

VICTORY IS NOT FOR THE LAZY

WITH THE MIDTERMS in the rearview mirror, I sought God for what was next and felt He gave me an analogy to help me think about and explain what is happening in America. As a country we are like a giant battleship that is starting to turn. God has already used Trump to annihilate laws and executive orders that for decades have handcuffed Christians and the church. For instance, Trump signed an executive order on May 4, 2017, that limited the enforcement of the Johnson Amendment. This amendment prohibited tax-exempt 501(c)(3) organizations from participating in political campaigning activities.[1] Under the Trump administration, the US Department of Health and Human Services issued a rule that exempts organizations from having to provide contraception coverage if they object to it on religious grounds.[2]

We can see righteousness being reinstituted, slowly but surely. Late-term abortions are being banned in many states. We are beginning to turn back to God as a nation. Though the fight is still fierce, the ship is starting to turn.

The critical point when a battleship is turning is the midpoint between its old position and the full turn. My father was in the navy, and he told me that a ship is most vulnerable to be attacked and sunk when it is midway in its turn. That is where we are right now as a nation. We are vulnerable because we are turning. The church—the praying church—is at the helm of this battleship because of our prayers and our agreement with heaven.

Only an ongoing commitment to prayer will keep that ship of state turning. God is restoring prayer to His church and this nation in so many ways. I believe many principles of prayer and faith were lost because the disciples were not attentive enough to Jesus' prayer habits. Remember that they fell asleep when Jesus was in the Garden of Gethsemane. They could have had a master class in the prayer life of the Messiah that night as He cried out in the hours before He would be crucified.

> Then Jesus came with them to a place called Gethsemane, and said to the disciples, "Sit here while I go and pray over there." And He took with Him Peter and the two sons of Zebedee, and He began to be sorrowful and deeply distressed. Then He said to them, "My soul is exceedingly sorrowful, even to death. Stay here and watch with Me."
>
> He went a little farther and fell on His face, and prayed, saying, "O My Father, if it is possible, let this cup pass from Me; nevertheless, not as I will, but as You will."
>
> Then He came to the disciples and found them sleeping, and said to Peter, "What! Could you not watch with Me one hour? Watch and pray, lest you

enter into temptation. The spirit indeed is willing, but the flesh is weak."

Again, a second time, He went away and prayed, saying, "O My Father, if this cup cannot pass away from Me unless I drink it, Your will be done." And He came and found them asleep again, for their eyes were heavy.

So He left them, went away again, and prayed the third time, saying the same words. Then He came to His disciples and said to them, "Are you still sleeping and resting? Behold, the hour is at hand, and the Son of Man is being betrayed into the hands of sinners. Rise, let us be going. See, My betrayer is at hand."

—MATTHEW 26:36–46

"Could you not watch with me one hour?" Those words ring throughout the centuries. I truly believe that if the disciples had stayed awake, they would have gained many insights about prayer that were lost or not understood. Because they didn't stay awake with Him, we don't have much of a record of how He prayed, what He said in his prayers, and the manner in which He prayed.

However, the Holy Spirit is in the business of restoring our understanding of prayer. He is enlightening hearts today and showing us our positions of power in the places of prayer. Prayer movements in the earth today—in South Korea, China, Latin America, and North America—are greater than any that have existed in history. Many books and courses and movements are dedicated to prayer, more than in previous decades. Christians who used to see prayer as being a little like pixie dust—toss it up in the air and hope something good happens—are realizing that wishes are not God's idea of faith-filled prayer. Rather, prayer is rooted in faith—the kind of faith God showed me in the five principles. These lessons on faith and on prayer are the very beginning of a new foundation that I believe will transform the church and this country.

One reason people don't pray more is because they don't see results from their prayers. This creates discouragement. God is presently giving His church extravagant examples of prayer that work mightily, and the elections of 2016 and 2018 are prime models. If you have felt discouraged that prayer doesn't change anything, the true accounts in this book should cause your hope and faith to soar. The Holy Spirit is doing much in our day through prayer. Can you feel it? It's your job to see it and connect with it—to join the corporate prayer movement rising in the nation and in your city.

My prayer is that this book will cause people to pray with new excitement, new expectation, and new hope. This book could be the catalyst that changes your family, your city, your church, and your life—forever.

PRAYING IN THE SPIRIT

One of the most empowering experiences in my life regarding prayer was being baptized in the Holy Spirit and being able to pray in the Spirit anytime I wanted. When I don't know what to pray, the Spirit in me does, and He prays through me in a language I can't understand with my mind, although my spirit bears witness that I am praying to God.

Before receiving this blessing, I used to wonder how it was possible that Paul said he could pray continually (1

Thess. 5:17). After receiving the fullness of the Holy Spirit, I gained that understanding. You really can pray continually, throughout the day, in the Holy Spirit. As I did this, I saw my prayer life go to another level.

I encourage everyone to seek the baptism of the fullness of the Holy Spirit with the prayer language God wants to give. It is a powerful way for our spirit man to make intercession. When we seek good things from God, He never gives us evil things. Jesus said, "If you then, being evil, know how to give good gifts to your children, how much more will your heavenly Father give the Holy Spirit to those who ask Him!" (Luke 11:13). If you ask Him for the baptism in the Holy Spirit, He will be faithful to give you the fullness of the Holy Spirit. This will become a beautiful way to enhance and empower your prayer life.

RESULTS ARE NOT FOR THE LAZY

Our nation has a day of prayer once a year, and I am thankful for that expression. But in the future that day of prayer will be much greater and deeper than it is presently. A true day of prayer in our country will look like what the prophet Joel wanted to see. It will include fasting, rending of hearts, repentance, and restoration of lost righteousness and holiness. Imagine the following biblical example taking place right here in the United States of America:

> Blow the trumpet in Zion, and sound an alarm in My holy mountain! Let all the inhabitants of the land tremble; for the day of the LORD is coming, for it is at

hand: a day of darkness and gloominess, a day of clouds and thick darkness, like the morning clouds spread over the mountains. A people come, great and strong, the like of whom has never been; nor will there ever be any such after them, even for many successive generations....

"Now, therefore," says the LORD, "Turn to Me with all your heart, with fasting, with weeping, and with mourning." So rend your heart, and not your garments; return to the LORD your God, for He is gracious and merciful, slow to anger, and of great kindness; and He relents from doing harm. Who knows if He will turn and relent, and leave a blessing behind Him—a grain offering and a drink offering for the LORD your God? Blow the trumpet in Zion, consecrate a fast, call a sacred assembly; gather the people, sanctify the congregation, assemble the elders, gather the children and nursing babes; let the bridegroom go out from his chamber, and the bride from her dressing room. Let the priests, who minister to the LORD, weep between the porch and the altar; let them say, "Spare Your people, O LORD, and do not give Your heritage to reproach, that the nations should rule over them. Why should they say among the peoples, 'Where is their God?'"

—JOEL 2:1–2, 12–17

Picture the people of God rising up and calling a day in which every believer, even the children, the newly married, the business leaders, the pastors, the ministry leaders, and all the laypeople rise up to weep and repent publicly. Can you imagine such a day happening in our lifetime? Can you see that God is building toward that day?

Of course, the enemy will mock and laugh at us every step of the way through the things he controls—some of the news media, entertainment venues, and academic institutions. But that goes with the territory and is already happening. The church is mocked daily in universities, capitols, and throughout much of the media. What else is new? Why not seek God with all our hearts as the prophet Joel wrote about so vividly? Why not put everything else aside and go for broke?

Some people want revival, but they don't like the discomfort it threatens to bring. They don't like the idea of fasting and repenting, let alone weeping and crying out publicly. I often hear people quote 2 Chronicles 7:14, the famous "if my people" passage. Let's look closely at what that actually says:

> Then the LORD appeared to Solomon by night, and said to him: "I have heard your prayer, and have chosen this place for Myself as a house of sacrifice. When I shut up heaven and there is no rain, or command the locusts to devour the land, or send pestilence among My people, if My people who are called by My name will humble themselves, and pray and seek My face, and *turn from their wicked ways*, then I will hear from heaven, and will forgive their sin and heal their land. Now My eyes will be open and My ears attentive to prayer made in this place. For now I have chosen and sanctified this house, that My name may be there forever; and My eyes and My heart will be there perpetually.
>
> —2 CHRONICLES 7:12-16, EMPHASIS ADDED

Notice that God refers to our "wicked ways." That phrase troubled me, and I asked the Holy Spirit, "What do you mean when You say to turn from our wicked ways? Man is sinful by nature. It is not possible while we remain in these sinful bodies for us to be completely free of sin in every single way. That is what forgiveness is for and why Jesus died for us on the cross. Your Word says we all fall short of the glory of God (Rom. 3:23), so turning from our wicked ways as a nation is bigger than I can believe for. I would love to believe for that, but I do not know if I really understand what You mean. Please explain this to me."

As I meditated on this scripture more, the Holy Spirit impressed on me to read the parable of the talents alongside this 2 Chronicles 7 passage. I turned to the familiar story Jesus told in the Gospels:

> For the kingdom of heaven is like a man traveling to a far country, who called his own servants and delivered his goods to them. And to one he gave five talents, to another two, and to another one, to each according to his own ability; and immediately he went on a journey. Then he who had received the five talents went and traded with them, and made another five talents. And likewise he who had received two gained two more also. But he who had received one went and dug in the ground, and hid his lord's money. After a long time the lord of those servants came and settled accounts with them.
>
> So he who had received five talents came and brought five other talents, saying, "Lord, you delivered to me five talents; look, I have gained five more talents besides them." His lord said to him, "Well done, good and faithful servant; you were faithful over a few things, I will make you ruler over many things. Enter into the

joy of your lord." He also who had received two talents came and said, "Lord, you delivered to me two talents; look, I have gained two more talents besides them." His lord said to him, "Well done, good and faithful servant; you have been faithful over a few things, I will make you ruler over many things. Enter into the joy of your lord."

Then he who had received the one talent came and said, "Lord, I knew you to be a hard man, reaping where you have not sown, and gathering where you have not scattered seed. And I was afraid, and went and hid your talent in the ground. Look, there you have what is yours."

But his lord answered and said to him, "You wicked and lazy servant, you knew that I reap where I have not sown, and gather where I have not scattered seed. So you ought to have deposited my money with the bankers, and at my coming I would have received back my own with interest. So take the talent from him, and give it to him who has ten talents.

"For to everyone who has, more will be given, and he will have abundance; but from him who does not have, even what he has will be taken away. And cast the unprofitable servant into the outer darkness. There will be weeping and gnashing of teeth."

—MATTHEW 25:14–30

Notice that the master called the lazy servant "wicked and slothful." It became crystal clear to me that God defines wickedness differently than we do. Yes, immorality, idolatry, greed, and so forth are wicked. But this servant exhibited none of these behaviors. His wickedness was of a different, subtler sort: he simply didn't want to go out of his way to do extra work. He didn't want to use the resources, abilities, and freedoms he had been given.

To God, laziness is wickedness.

Think about how God put Adam and Eve in a perfect garden to tend to it. He created them (and us) for partnership, and He put assignments in their hands to do. I know that many of us work hard, but I think we have defined laziness in a way that lets ourselves off the hook. Many Christian Americans rely on the government, employee benefits, pensions, or retirement investments to do everything for us when we should be relying on God. As believers we have gotten lazy. We seem to do all the right things—go to church, tithe, be good—but we have become wicked by standing on the sidelines, expecting everything to come to us. We have been lulled into the kind of complacency that God defines as wickedness.

I hope you're feeling the ouch of that.

To enjoy our freedoms in this country and not pray fervently for it is, by definition, laziness. It is wicked. Perhaps the great wickedness in the church in our day is passivity, an unwillingness to engage our time and energy in the public sphere. We live life unto ourselves, indulging in our prosperity and physical safety, while our country heads in exactly the wrong direction. We as the church cannot blame anybody but ourselves for the condition of the world. We are supposed to be salt and light in the world. We need to engage our culture in the realms of education, politics, government, entertainment, and more. But we fear offending people, experiencing public disapproval on social media or in the office, and losing our jobs for speaking up. So we don't speak up. We don't defend what the Word of God says is righteous.

We love the blessings of God, but when was the last time we threw ourselves wholeheartedly into prayer and fasting, rending our garments, and repenting for the immorality and godlessness gripping so many parts or our nation? When does that show up on the church calendar?

It must enter our thinking that God is offended by our wicked laziness more than people are offended by our speaking up on issues of the day. Whose disapproval do we prefer, theirs or His? Whose lasts longer?

Let me ask all of us: What does an active, engaged, faith-filled church look like? It certainly begins with prayer. I want to echo the prophet Joel's words and call everyone reading these words to pray, to call on others to prayer, and to pray in line with the Word of God. Pray for those who are in authority over us. Pray for our president, for our congressmen, for our senators, for our governors, and for our local government leaders. Pray for the school board, county leaders, sheriffs, judges, and every elected position whose term of service goes before the people.

Pray that the Spirit of God will permeate our leaders' hearts and minds to vote and legislate in line with the will of God. Pray that the kingdom of heaven will dominate our politics and our society in all areas. Pray that His will is done on earth as it is in heaven. Just praying these things day after day will open your eyes to see the awakening that is about to hit our country. Pray for your family. Pray for the youth in this nation to be set free from bondages, lies, and the moral confusion being fed to them in schools and society. Pray for clarity and revelation in the minds of people young and old. God can do this!

Prayer is the first thing, but not the only thing. We must reject laziness, get off our couches, and show up at council meetings and school board meetings and make our voices heard. We must volunteer to work in some of these venues. Work the polling places. Go down to the voting booth. Don't be lazy and wait for someone else to do it, for that is wickedness. If you have the power and ability, you will answer for what you did with every opportunity to use that power.

God may very well be waiting for you to be that righteous person He calls to run for office, to run for a position you may never have considered. Age does not matter. Whether you are eighteen or ninety-eight, you can engage and be a part of what God wants to do in this earth and in this country. We will be amazed in the days to come by the nobodies who become somebodies because they believed that God could use anybody.

When God's people stop letting the wickedness of laziness and passivity define our Christian experience, schedules, energy, and priorities, then the prayer movement will shift into another gear. We will become the answer to many of the prayers we have been praying.

Our reward is to forever be known as good and faithful servants in the eyes of God (Matt. 25:21). Wow! Our victory goes far beyond political gain and societal change. The very approval of God in the ages to come is in the balance.

For my part, I have already given God my yes for whatever He wants me to do in the elections that are ahead. I will do it for Him, for my children and grandchildren, and for this country. I don't want Him to have to send a stranger from another state to my office to talk sense into me again. I want to have a soft heart, untainted by laziness or unwillingness. I am going to spend myself for the purposes of God in my generation with all the time I have left.

I want you to join me. I want this book to spur you and inspire you and give you practical wisdom to illuminate your part in God's plans for this country through the body of Christ. Ask Him in the cool of the day and all throughout the day what He wants you to accomplish for His kingdom. Ask Him to direct your path, to show you His purpose for your life—why He has put you here, now, for such a time as this.

Then be encouraged to do your part. In the days and elections to come, let us stand in agreement and believe that the Spirit of God is indeed turning our ship of state, bringing about a great awakening not only in this country, but around the world. Let us watch the hand of God move upon our politics and politicians, on our entertainers and news reporters, sports figures, intellectuals, and more. Whatever we experience in the form of persecution and attacks, let it come. Together as a body of believers, we will declare the principles of faith and the principles of His everlasting Word, standing hand in hand, knitted heart to heart, working for the victorious future God has in store for this great nation.

May the Spirit of the Lord enlighten each of us beyond what He has revealed in these pages, and may the greatest stories of our lives be ahead of us as we rise to our destiny as individuals and as a nation. Amen!

To join us for prayer calls in future elections,
*visit **www.marycolbert.us***
and become part of our movement.

A movie called The Trump Prophecy *was made about
the prayer call I hosted for the 2016 election. The movie
was in theaters, and you can obtain the DVD online.*

☸ Notes ☸

Chapter 2
The Principle of Faith in Constant Motion

1. Adam Eliyahu Berkowitz, "Did Scientists Just Confirm Biblical Account of Sodom and Gomorrah?" Breaking Israel News, November 23, 2018, https://www.breakingisraelnews.com/117449/scientists-confirm-sodom-gomorrah/.

Chapter 3
The Principle of Faith That Excites God

1. Behind the Name, s.v. "John," accessed December 17, 2019, https://www.behindthename.com/name/john.

2. Behind the Name, s.v. "Trump," accessed December 17, 2019, https://surnames.behindthename.com/name/trump/submitted.

3. Dictionary.com, s.v. "trump," accessed December 17, 2019, https://www.dictionary.com/browse/trump; Online Etymology Dictionary, s.v. "trump," accessed December 17, 2019, https://www.etymonline.com/word/trump.

Chapter 8
God Leads Us in Triumph

1. Larry Huch's teaching on the shofar is used here with permission.

2. "Six-Day War: The Liberation of the Temple Mount and the Western Wall (June 7, 1967)," Jewishvirtuallibrary.org, accessed November 20, 2019, https://www.jewishvirtuallibrary.org/the-liberation-of-the-temple-mount-and-western-wall-june-1967.

3. Fox News, "Fox News Projects: Donald Trump Wins Wisconsin, Iowa," YouTube, November 8, 2015, https://www.youtube.com/watch?v=JVBfaH-Qedw; Chris Ladd, "How the Blue Wall Cracked," *Forbes*, November 21, 206, https://www.forbes.com/sites/chrisladd/2016/11/21/how-the-blue-wall-cracked/.

CHAPTER 10
PRAYING WITH POWER

1. Phil Helsel, "Dennis Hof, Nevada Brothel Owner and Assembly Candidate, Died of Heart Attack," NBC Universal, March 28, 2019, https://www.nbcnews.com/news/us-news/dennis-hof-nevada-brothel-owner-assembly-candidate-died-heart-attack-n988721.

CHAPTER 11
VICTORY IS NOT FOR THE LAZY

1. "President Trump Signs 'Johnson Amendment' Executive Order Limiting Treasury's Actions Against Religious Organizations Engaged in Political Campaign Activities," National Law Forum, May 10, 2017, https://www.natlawreview.com/article/president-trump-signs-johnson-amendment-executive-order-limiting-treasury-s-actions.

2. Jacqueline Howard, "Trump Administration Weakens Obamacare Birth Control Coverage Mandate," Cable News Network, November 7, 2018, https://www.cnn.com/2018/11/07/health/birth-control-exemption-trump-bn/index.html.

1. Faith must be in constant motion.

2. Have the kind of faith that excites God!

3. Faith is the Substance of things

Made in the USA
Middletown, DE
09 October 2020

21516266R00086